Bridging the Divide:
Group work for social justice

I0127566

Proceedings of the XL International Symposium
of the International Association for Social Work with Groups,
Skukuza, Kruger National Park, South Africa

Bridging the Divide:
Group work for social justice

Edited by
Reineth Prinsloo and Janetta Ananias

w&b

MMXXI

© Whiting & Birch Ltd 2021
Published by Whiting & Birch Ltd,
Forest Hill, London SE23 3HZ
ISBN 9781861776280

Contents

**Proceedings of the XL International Symposium
of the International Association for Social Work with Groups,
Skukuza, Kruger National Park, South Africa**

Acknowledgements

**Proceedings of the XL International Symposium
of the International Association for Social Work with Groups,
Skukuza, Kruger National Park, South Africa**

Symposium International Honoree
Reineth Prinsloo

Symposium Local Honorees
SizaBantwana
Funanani
Lizzy Mashimbye
Rita Wasserman

Posthumous Honoree
Winnie Madikizela-Mandela

Symposium Planner
Emily Wilk

Symposium Chair and Coordinator of Local Planning
Reineth Prinsloo

We would like to thank Prof Antoinette Lombard, the Head of the Department of Social Work and Criminology at the University of Pretoria, the Employee Wellness office of the South African National Parks at Skukuza, and Distell (www.distell.co.za) for their support of the 2018 IASWG Symposium.

The planning of the symposium would not have been possible without the diligent administration and support of Emily Wilk. She is an indispensable asset to IASWG, and we are extremely grateful to have had her on board. We also thank the 56 student volunteers from around the world who assisted in the smooth organising of the symposium.

Without the submissions of the authors included in this Proceedings and the diligence of the reviewers who assisted in the process, this publication would not have been possible. Thank you to everyone who contributed. Thank you to Phil Botha for editing the document.

Thank you also to Greg Tully, President of IASWG at the time of the symposium, for his constant support of the South Africa Symposium and his unfailing belief that we would be able to host the event.

Local Symposium Planning Committee

Academic
Sub-themes Creation; Marketing; Abstract Review:
Louie Claasen UNISA, Roshini Pillay WITS, Janet Ananias UNAM

Continuous Professional Development
Poppy Masinga

IT and Design Support
Conrad Prinsloo, Paul Prinsloo

On-Site Registration
Jacqui Dunn

Practice
Community Visit and Outreach:
Hilda Baar, Lenie Galloway, Jaco Lubbe, Frank Mashego,
Sherlock Shabangu, Rita Wasserman, Mari Wasserman

Student Volunteers
Kristen Perron, Christia Potgieter, Charlotte Sibanyoni

Support and Administration
Mari Wasserman, Gert Prinsloo

Symposium Bags
Minky Mashego, Mari Wasserman, Elmarie van der Merwe,
Example Valoyi

About the Editors

Reineth Prinsloo, DPhil, MSW, BSW, is an Associate Professor in the Department of Social Work and Criminology, Faculty of Humanities, at the University of Pretoria in South Africa. She teaches Family Development and Guidance and social work with groups. She specialises in marriage and family preservation and growth groups, based on a strength perspective. Reineth is the Vice-President of the International Association for Social Work with Groups (IASWG). One of her current research focuses is on group work and social enterprises with arts and crafts within a developmental welfare approach. Another research focus is multicultural and social justice competence in group work, an area in which she has been invited as a keynote speaker to several symposiums. She published nationally and internationally on social work with groups. Email: reineth.prinsloo@up.ac.za

Janetta Ananias, PhD, is Senior Lecturer and Head of the Department of Social Work at the University of Namibia. She has 16 years of teaching experience in social work and has taught a wide range of areas such as social work with groups, social welfare law, and social gerontology. She also has social work practice experience in mental health, substance abuse, child and family care, and HIV/AIDS. She has published widely and presented papers at several national and international conferences. She has been a member of the International Association of Social Work with Groups (IASWG) for the past five years. Email: jananias@unam.na

About the Contributors

Information about the authors as well as the reviewers for the Proceedings is presented.

Janetta Ananias, PhD, is Senior Lecturer and Head of the Department of Social Work at the University of Namibia. She has 16 years of teaching experience in social work and has taught a wide range of areas such as social work with groups, social welfare law, and social gerontology. She also has social work practice experience in mental health, substance abuse, child and family care, and HIV/AIDS. She has published widely and presented papers at several national and international conferences. She has been a member of the International Association of Social Work with Groups (IASWG) for the past five years. Email: jananias@unam.na

Hilda Baar-Kooij, EdD, is a licensed group worker and educator in the Netherlands, who uses her GISSKID programme with schools and teachers to raise awareness of the difference between "handing over knowledge" and "facilitating learning," internalised and integrated knowledge, and what transpires in groups. She trains teachers in group work knowledge and skills to address problems like bullying, cyberbullying or conflicts stemming from cultural differences. Email: hjbaar@gmail.com

Noa Barkai-Kra is a social worker and lecturer in the Social Work Department at Ben-Gurion University, and a social work school at the Ashkelon Academic College, with a BA and MA in Social Work from Ben-Gurion University, specialising in creative tools and community work for social change. She is now in the final stages of her doctoral study on the subject "Creative tools as a bridge in binational groups." During the last 10 years, along with teaching at the academy, Noa has been conducting workshops and courses for Arab-Jewish conflict/ dialogue groups on behalf of Neve Shalom. She presents short-term and long-term workshops for youth, teachers, and adults as well as social activist courses, working with creative tools in social work. Email: noabarkai@gmail.com

Leigh Ann Salonika Namdis Black is a social work practitioner employed by the Directorate of Developmental Social Welfare Services in the Ministry of Health and Social Services, Namibia. She holds a

BA (Honours) Social Work degree from the University of Namibia. She has eight years of practice experience in the areas of suicide prevention and substance abuse prevention and treatment. Her work with older persons involved screening of older persons for placements in residential care facilities and the supervision of such facilities. Her research and practice interest in institutional and community-based care for older persons led to the initiative of support groups for caregivers of older persons. Email: leigh009@gmail.com

Elmien Claassens, MSW, is a practice lecturer in the Department of Social Work and Criminology at the University of Pretoria, South Africa, since 2019. Before that, she practised in the community development arena for approximately 20 years. She was the CEO of a non-profit organization that rendered services in communities in and around Tshwane, Pretoria, South Africa. The focus of the organisation was early-childhood education, primary school education and support to the families of children in educational programmes. The integration of practice teaching and exposure of students on the ground level in communities remains one of her passions. Email: elmienclaassens@gmail.com

Mark Doel, PhD, CQSW, is Emeritus Professor at Sheffield Hallam University (SHU), England. He is a registered social worker with twenty years of community-based social work experience during which he specialised in groupwork, practice education and task-centred practice. Mark has lived and worked in the US as a caseworker and a Principal Investigator. He has been a Practice Educator, Head of School, and a Research Professor. He has led several projects in Russia and Eastern Europe, helping to establish the first social work education programmes in Georgia. Mark is widely published and has encouraged many authors in his role as past co-editor of the *Groupwork* journal. Mark has been Vice-President of the International Association for Social Work with Groups (IASWG); is Honorary Professor at Tbilisi State University Georgia; and a Visiting Scholar at the University of Pretoria, South Africa. Email: markdoel@icloud.com

Jennie Fleming is currently Co-Director of Practical Participation. Until November 2013 she was Director of the Centre for Social Action and Reader in Participatory Research and Social Action at De Montfort University, where she led participatory research and evaluation projects. Jennie is an experienced, internationally renowned groupworker, researcher and trainer, committed to working in a participative and empowering way with difficult to engage groups. At the time of presenting the paper at the IASWG symposium, she was Editor of the *Groupwork* journal and on the Board of the IASWG. She is a Visiting Fellow at Nottingham Trent University. With Dave Ward, Jennie has co-edited *Social action and self-directed groupwork* (Whiting and Birch, 2019), and co-authored with Audrey Mullender, *Empowerment In Action: Self-Directed Groupwork* (Palgrave, 2013). Email: jennie.fleming@ntu.ac.uk

Lorrie Greenhouse Gardella, JD, LMSW, ACSW, is an Associate Professor of Social Work and MSW Program Coordinator at Southern Connecticut State University in New Haven, Connecticut, USA. Introduced to social group work as a settlement house volunteer, she served as a consultant in children's law before earning her MSW degree. She has published in the areas of social group work, social work with migrants, and social work history, including the acclaimed biography, *The Life and Thought of Louis Lowy: Social Work through the Holocaust* (Syracuse University Press, 2011), which was recently published in German (Lambertus Verlag, 2019). Having held leadership positions in various social work associations, she is proud to serve as a member-at-large on the IASWG Board of Directors and as co-chair of the International Issues Committee. Email: lggardella@gmail.com

Ephrat Huss is a professor of Social Work at the Ben-Gurion University of the Negev where she chairs an innovative MA in Art therapy for social workers. She has published extensively on arts in social work and on arts-based research in social work research. She is now working on an Israeli Science Foundation grant on using arts-based research to understand and intensify coping of impoverished Bedouin youth. She is currently researching arts as embodied pedagogy in social work, autogenic coping through arts, and she has set up and researched an arts-based youth group for Arab and Jewish youth in the south of Israel. She is at present researching psychosocial interventions with refugees in Lesbos and editing a book on arts to transform society and on arts-based research in social practice. Email: ehuss@bgu.ac.il

Paul Johnson, DSW, LCSW is a Professor in the School of Social Work at the University of Southern Maine. He taught at Lehman College from 1996-1999 and has taught at USM for the past 21 years. Paul has taught in Social Work Practice, Social Welfare Policy, Research, Fieldwork and Groupwork. Before his academic career, he worked in New York City at the Jewish Child Care Association from 1988 to 1995 and United

Cerebral Palsy of New York State from 1986-1988. Before moving to the United States in 1986, he worked in Intake and Residential Social Work in the United Kingdom. He has published extensively and presented at numerous national and international conferences. He has been a member of (IASWG) since 1997, and for the past 10 years has been a member of the Editorial Board of Groupwork. Email: paulj@maine.edu

Leanne Jordaan, BSW, MSW, is a social work lecturer in the Department of Social Work and Criminology, University of Pretoria, South Africa. After ten years in the field of Employee Wellness, she shifted her focus towards working with children in schools, a field in which she obtained her MSW (with specialisation in Play Therapy) with a focus on work with adolescents. She currently works in the field of social work practice education with first and final year social work students. Email: leanne.jordaan@up.ac.za

Sarah LaRocque, PhD, MSW, RSW, is a clinician in community mental health specialising in group work and complex trauma. She is a sessional instructor in the Faculty of Social Work, University of Calgary, Canada. She is an active group researcher with the University of Calgary and acts as a liaison with social scientists from various disciplines, bringing research into clinical settings to support research-informed practice and scientist-practitioner collaborations. She has published on group education and training and has presented at regional, national, and international conferences on group work. As a field instructor, she developed a group training method for social work students in practicum. She is a past president of the Calgary Section of the Canadian Group Psychotherapy Association (CGPA) and past National Secretary. Email: slarocqu@ucalgary.ca

Georg Nebel was a graduated social worker and certified social group worker, co-founder of the Institute for Advice and Supervision in Aachen, Germany. He was a community worker, group dynamist and NLP master, organizational developer, supervisor for the "Deutsche Gesellschaft für systemische Supervision" and teacher of supervision at the "Systemische Gesellschaft." Until 2018, he oversaw the intensive advanced training in social group work at the Institute for Advice and Supervision. He was one of the founders of the German chapter of the IASWG and served on the board until 2000. He was instrumental in the development of the chapter into a professional organisation and the certification of group workers. Over the years, Nebel trained and inspired generations of group workers in Germany. He was the co-editor and co-publisher of the book *"Werkbuch für das Arbeiten mit Gruppen,"* an essential resource for all group workers since it not only furthers the development of the theory of group phases to a circular understanding of the background of the autopoiesis of groups as living or social systems but also contains a remarkable compilation of resource-oriented, methodical interventions in groups. He died on March 18, 2020.

Ulrike Overs arbeitete zunächst als Erzieherin und Montessori-Pädagogin in einem Montessori-Kinderhaus in Aachen, Deutschland und war als Honorarkraft im Bereich Erwachsenenbildung tätig. Mit den Schwerpunkten Kleinkindpädagogik und musikalische Früherziehung gab sie Fortbildungen für Eltern und Erzieherinnen und leitete Eltern-Kind-Gruppen. Auf dem 2. Bildungsweg studierte sie soziale Arbeit an der Katholischen Fachhochschule Aachen mit dem Abschluss Diplom Sozialpädagogin und nahm an der Intensivfortbildung "Social Groupwork" teil, die sie mit einem Zertifikat abschloss. Nebenberuflich hat sie immer mal wieder Gruppen über einen längeren Zeitraum geteamt. Seit 15 Jahren ist sie im Bereich Gemeinwesenarbeit tätig und arbeitet für die evangelische und katholische Kirchengemeinde im Aachener Westen. Zu ihren Aufgaben gehören die Koordination und Leitung des Stadtteilnetzwerkes Netzanschluss, des sozialen Cafés mit Kleiderlädchen und seit etwa 3 Jahren der Aufbau einer ressourcenorientierten Seniorenarbeit "Engagiert älter werden in Aachen West." Email: u.overs@netzanschluss.org

Roshini Pillay (South Africa) was educated at the University of the Western Cape (PhD), with an MA in EAP from the University of Pretoria, an Honours in Industrial Psychology from UNISA and a Bachelor of Social Work (BSW) from the University of KwaZulu Natal. She has worked in the field of social work for 20 years before lecturing at the University of the Witwatersrand from 2009 to date. She was the recipient of the Thuthuka Grant. Roshini has published in the field of social work education and group work. She has presented at local and international conferences. She is a member of the International Association of Social Work with Groups and has taught group work to undergraduate and postgraduate social work students. Email: roshini.pillay@wits.ac.za

Reineth Prinsloo, DPhil, MSW, BSW, is an Associate Professor in the Department of Social Work and Criminology, Faculty of Humanities, at the University of Pretoria, South Africa. She teaches

Family Development and Guidance and Social Work with Groups. She specialises in marriage and family preservation and growth groups, based on a strength perspective. Reineth is the Vice-President of the International Association for Social Work with Groups (IASWG). One of her current research focuses is on group work and social enterprises with arts and crafts within a developmental welfare approach. Another research focus is multicultural and social justice competence in group work, an area in which she has been invited as a keynote speaker to several symposiums. She published nationally and internationally on social work with groups. Email: reineth.prinsloo@up.ac.za

Gerda Reitsma, PhD, MSc, HED, is Associate Professor at the North-West University in Potchefstroom, South Africa. She is the Director of the Centre for Health Professions Education. She is a 2017 FAIMER/SAFRI fellow, and a member of AMEE and ISSoTL. She is a board member of the Sub-Saharan Interprofessional Education Network (AfrIPEN) and the Southern African Health Educationalist Association (SAAHE). Her research involves innovation in health professions education, including active learning methodologies and blended learning. She is among others responsible for mentorship and faculty development in the Faculty of Health Sciences to promote Scholarship of Teaching and Learning. Email: gerda.reitsma@nwu.ac.za

Mamadou Seck is an Associate Professor at the School of Social Work, Cleveland State University (CSU), USA. He started as an elementary school headmaster in a large village where he was among the first individuals to be contacted for help. This experience inspired him to take the entrance exam to the National School of Social Work in Senegal to become a social worker with delinquent and at-risk youth. He was selected by the Council of International Programs (CIP) and joined the United States for training at the Ohio Department of Youth Services. He earned a Master of Science in Social Administration and a PhD at Case Western Reserve University. He writes on juvenile justice, social work education and student success, group work, developmental disability, and economic and social development. His collaboration with the School of Specialized Social Workers in Dakar, Senegal, enabled him to write on social group work intervention in rural areas. Currently, Dr Seck is the Faculty Fellow for Civic Engagement at CSU where he teaches Fundamentals of Social Work Research and Advanced Generalist Group Work. He is the Chair of the NE-Ohio Chapter of the IASWG. Email: mamadouseck@att.net

Greg Tully, Ph.D., MSW, is a tenured Professor in Social Work at West Chester University in Pennsylvania, USA. He also teaches courses for the Silver School of Social Work at New York University (NYU). He has been Departmental Chairperson and a tenured faculty member at Iona College (New York, USA), an Associate Professor at Barry University (Florida, USA), and has taught courses at the Hunter College Silberman School of Social Work (New York USA). He has presented internationally, and published books and articles including contributions to the *Encyclopedia of Social Work with Groups,* the *Journal of Teaching in Social Work, Groupwork,* and *Social Work with Groups.* He is a Board Member (as recent President) of the International Association for Social Work with Groups (IASWG). Email: gtully@wcupa.edu

Marie Ubbink, PhD (SW), MA (Soc), Bed (Orto), BASW is Associate Professor in the School of Psychosocial Science in the Subject group Social Work at the North-West University, Potchefstroom, South Africa. She started her social work teaching career in 2011. She specialises in group work and teaches the method for undergraduate social work students. Her research involves group work and she was principal investigator on an empowering narrative leadership group work program for disadvantaged communities in South African. She guides postgraduate students in group work projects and is an external examiner for social work postgraduate students. She is a member of the International Association for Social Work with Groups (IASWG). Email: marie.ubbink@nwu.ac.za

Dave Ward is Professor of Social and Community Studies at De Montfort University, Leicester, UK. His interests lie in groupwork and in work with offenders, particularly young people in trouble, about which he has researched and published extensively. In particular, he has focussed on the application, through groupwork, of the values and methods of transformative education (Paulo Freire) to practice, training, research, teamwork, and management. In recognition of his contribution to groupwork, Dave has been made International Honoree by the International Association for the Advancement of Social Work with Groups. Dave and Jennie Fleming co-edited *Social action and self-directed groupwork* (Whiting and Birch, 2019), and co-authored with Audrey Mullender, *Empowerment in Action: Self-Directed Groupwork* (Palgrave, 2013). Email: dward@dmu.ac.uk

Gerna Wessels, BSW, MSW and DPhil, is a senior lecturer in the Department of Social Work and Criminology at the University of Pretoria, South-Africa. She is responsible for coordinating the practice education component of the Department and has been involved in practice teaching on first, third and final year levels for the past 30 years. She is a member of the IASWG. Email: gerna.wessels@up.ac.za

Christine Wilkins, Ph.D., LCSW is the Advance Care Planning Program Manager at New York University (NYU) Langone Health, Adjunct Faculty at NYU Silver School of Social Work, and Clinical Assistant Professor at NYU Grossman School of Medicine. She has taught core clinical social work courses, including clinical practice with groups, and advised students for the past 18 years. She has presented nationally and internationally on clinical social work, social group work, advance care planning, program development, domestic violence, and palliative care. She was co-chair for the 2016, 2017, and 2019 IASWG International Symposia in New York City. She served as member-at-large and Symposium Committee co-chair on the IASWG and member-at-large on the NASW-NYC Board of Directors. Email: Christine.Wilkins@nyulangone.org

Introduction

We dream of a better world, of equal opportunities for all, of making a difference, and of creating awareness. We dreamed of bringing the world to South Africa. These dreams were at the core of conceptualising the theme for the 2018 symposium, and June 2018 saw the dreams become a reality. We were immensely proud that IASWG chose South Africa to host the celebratory 40th annual symposium.

Bridging divides has many meanings. As the members of the IASWG organisation celebrated their 40th international symposium in South Africa, it was our view that the 2018 symposium theme of "Bridging the Divide: Group Work for Social Justice" was an appropriate and relevant theme in the global environment. At the core of social group work is the need to bridge the divide to develop mutual aid and to foster a socially just society where all members have the same opportunities to attain material goods, income, and wealth.

The valuing of diverse perspectives and experiences is a heartfelt call to understanding the meaning of *Ubuntu* in South Africa and all of Africa. *Ubuntu* is about humaneness, and it embraces values of respect, solidarity, community development, social responsibility, justice, and equality. That said, bridging the divide, in our view, suggests more than just an appreciation of diversity. It is a real recognition of being part of humanity. Bridging the divide for social justice is about people living and working in a globalised society brought together with a common group purpose. The South Africa symposium contributed to the social and economic development of our people – a tangible act of social justice!

The contributions in the Proceedings are from Canada, Germany, Israel, the United States, Namibia and South Africa and attest to the importance of social work with groups as a tool to bridge divides for social justice. We pay tribute to Georg Nebel, a founding member of the German Chapter, who died in March 2020. Georg was an activist for group work and was instrumental in establishing the IASWG Chapter in Germany. We acknowledge his contribution and pay our respects in the tribute.

Fifty-six student volunteers from the United States, Namibia and South Africa assisted in the on-site management of the symposium.

Apart from their management duties they bonded as a group and engaged in intense group discussions about social work and the intricacies of the world through the eyes of young adults and social workers in the making. Christele Lloyd, a South African student volunteer, wrote a poignant poem about her experience of *Ubuntu* in the connections and presented it at the closing ceremony. Paul Johnson penned his experience of the symposium down in his personal recollection of getting on the plane in the US to departing back home. According to Paul, the symposium opened opportunities for networking and bonding and provided experiences of the immense beauty of diversity – in cultures, backgrounds, languages, experiences, nature, and having fun.

****

The symposium opened with a workshop by Lorrie Gardella and Reineth Prinsloo which is discussed in the chapter, "Build the Social Justice Bridge: participatory photography with the international group work community." The chapter discusses a participatory photography project where social work students, educators, and practitioners from around the world contributed photographs and brief narratives that represented the relationship between group work and social justice. In the opening workshop more than 200 participants from ten countries reflected on the meaning of the photos for the group work community. In viewing the photos, symposium participants identified a common vision of social justice as well as culturally specific approaches to group work. Implications are drawn for the internationalisation of professional knowledge.

Poverty results from inadequate access to resources. Gerna Wessels and Elmien Claassens discuss the role of social work with groups in dealing with poverty. Poverty alleviation projects may cause recipients of the services to feel dissatisfied, embarrassed, and unwilling to participate. This feeds into the perception that people living in poverty do not want to change their circumstances. It is the responsibility of social service providers to use different ways to address poverty in a dignified manner, not disregarding the capabilities of people living in poverty. Through empowerment group work, group members can be allowed to have their voices heard regarding projects designed to provide them with opportunities for upward mobility. This paper discusses a poverty alleviation project where service-users are active partners.

Poverty is an international problem, as Ulrike Overs discusses in her contribution on community work and group work to assist single mothers with a low income in Germany. Her chapter describes the establishment and development of a district network for single parents and their children, which was launched about 15 years ago in Aachen, Germany. This was initiated in the west of Aachen by the Catholic and Protestant parishes, each of which saw a need for action. In order to understand the motivation of the initiators, the situation of single parents in Germany is discussed, first, the risk of falling into (relative) poverty is described, and second, the living situation of many single parents in Germany receives attention.

Roshini Pillay and Sarah LaRocque examine their teaching methods in social work with groups to undergraduate and post-graduate students in Canada and South Africa. In this chapter, mutual considerations such as social justice, respect for diversity and the use of a strengths-based approach are used so that students may apply skills and techniques in group work. A theoretical foundation using situated cognitive learning and apprenticeship is suggested for interrogating how real-world factors contribute to knowledge and skill acquisition in group work education. The South African educator offers ways of using the principles of authentic learning in the theory of group work for course design. The Canadian educator illustrates how field education can be infused with participant observation and research-informed learning to provide foundational instruction in the real world. Through the lens of these educators, the theory and field practice in group work are explored in a novel and pedagogical sound manner.

Group work education receives further attention in the chapter by Marié Ubbink and Gerda Reitsma. The authors emphasise that many students attending university face challenges based on their background and the unfamiliar university context, and they struggle to cope in the university learning environment. These students need support in the classroom in the form of social networking and peer support. By creating an environment where students can learn with each other and from each other, the possibility for these students to survive and thrive in a university setting increases. Team-Based Learning (TBL) promotes collaborative learning through effective group work. In this chapter, the application of TBL in a social work module is discussed. Students learn how to work in groups effectively, and how to apply group work techniques in practice. An additional advantage of implementing TBL is that students guide and support each other to complete tasks, thus creating an environment where students who experience challenges in other environments can function and achieve their learning goals.

Mamadou Seck provides yet another group work method in teaching social work students through his paper on Rapid Rural Participatory Research Methodology for understanding human behaviours in a social environment, a method used by many African schools of social work. The training offers students an opportunity to review the content of their group work courses as they re-examine in live situations group work principles and processes, stages of group development, group cohesion, and evaluation of members' interactions, leadership, conflicts, and problem solving. Further, it enhances their skills in time management and task completion when involved in community development interventions. This practice-focused chapter describes the theoretical workshop and field practice stages of a training session designed to assess a village's potentials but also its residents' needs and management of the natural resources. It further describes opportunities the training session provides to study the types of interactions that bridge the divide between sedentary and nomadic residents as well as that between rural and urban populations. In addition, implications for practice, advocacy and policy, and research are outlined.

Social justice requires access to resources for all age groups. Leanne Jordaan reminds the reader of the power of group work in promoting social justice for older persons. Group work, as a social work intervention method, was repeatedly shown to be an efficient way of successfully working with older persons. However, as a practice educator it was noted that attempts at meaningful interventions with older persons were often limited or did not achieve the desired outcome. However, when the students used group work focusing on the older persons' need to continue to make valuable contributions in society, the interventions were both meaningful and well-received by the recipients. Whilst completing practice work at a residential care facility for older persons in Pretoria, South Africa, a student social worker developed an intergenerational skills-transfer programme which had group work as the central point of the intervention. The use of group work broke down preconceived ideas of work with older persons and created an opportunity to offer quality services to older persons in the residential care facility.

The focus shifts to community-based care of older people in urban and rural settings in Namibia and how this serves to bridge the divide. Janetta Ananias and Leigh Ann Black highlight the fact that many older people worldwide live in the community rather than in institutional settings and are cared for by their families. With the breakdown of the extended family system and the high costs of institutional care for older persons, there have been increasing calls for community-based interventions to enhance the care of older people. This chapter describes a community-based programme for caregivers of older persons that was aimed at enhancing the quality of care provided by informal caregivers of older people in an urban and rural setting in Namibia. The support group programme equipped informal caregivers with knowledge about aging and caregiving. Also, coping skills and support were offered with a positive impact on the knowledge of, and a sense of support amongst, informal caregivers.

Intimate partner violence is a life-threatening public health problem. Michael Lyman, Cheyenne Port, Michelle Cousins, Emily Stottlemyer, Monica DeCarlo, Paige Bankhead-Lewis, and Adolfo Alvarez present the contribution of a group work program for intimate partner violence perpetrators. One of the approaches to addressing this serious social justice issue is to intervene with the perpetrators of such violence through a group-based Batterer Intervention Program. The chapter discusses the AMEND program in the United States and its efforts to reduce recidivism rates for intimate partner violence perpetrators. The program does not focus on anger management but takes a feminist psychoeducational approach focusing on power and control, using feedback of fellow perpetrators in group work contexts to assist in the intervention process. The mutual aid received in the group, as well as feedback from other group members, thus add another dimension to the intervention process.

The chapter, "Populism: a challenge for group work" by Jennie Fleming and Dave Ward seeks to extend our understanding of the notion of populism and its resonance with the democratic values of group work. The authors continued to explore the social action and self-directed model and how it can be useful in responses to populism. As a further illustration, the authors provided practical examples of how self-directed group work can be used to challenge the terrain of populism.

Group work to address the Arab-Israeli conflict is presented in the chapter, "Using arts as a contact method in group work with latency age Arab and Jewish youth in Israel" by Noa Barkai and Ephrat Huss. In a case study, arts activities were used to create positive interactions amongst the youth utilising an action-based approach. The contact theory was drawn on to facilitate encounters between conflicting youth groups. Amongst the interesting findings was the complexity in enhancing contact and fun amongst the youth while continued stereotypes and discomfort persisted. A question which remains unanswered, however, is how to address racism, othering, and political contact in group work.

In memoriam: Georg Nebel

Georg Nebel acted as a reviewer for the 2018 IASWG Symposium Proceedings. We acknowledge his assistance in this regard and his tremendous contribution to group work as a method in social work. The German Chapter pays tribute.

On March 18, 2020, our dear friend and teacher Georg Nebel died after a long illness. With Georg, a great teacher of social group work has left us. We even might say that he was one of the founding fathers of social group work in Germany. The development of the Aachen curriculum for intensive training in social groupwork, is the special merit of Georg Nebel.

Georg was a practitioner who, with his skills, his professionalism, but above all with his personality, inspired and trained many group workers in Germany.

Georg was one of the social workers who first learned a "decent job." Like many of his generation, he always stood with both feet in life. When he designed the curriculum for the intensive training for group workers, it was not because he considered starting a new school for social work, but because of his "down to earth" attitude, making him understand how group work is one of the essential and most potent methods of social work in all work fields. That did not make him a blind pragmatist. He received the first impression of group work through group dynamics. However, he did not perceive the basic psychoanalytic attitude to social work as adequate in all fields.

Georg also studied the method of community work which commonly used group work. For Georg, group work in the context of community work often was focussed on the identification of local leaders. This was a too narrow view in his perspective since it did not use the potential of the group members.

With the theories on social work with groups, as taught at the Boston University, the systemic constructivism as an epistemological basis came to Germany, especially through Louis Lowy. Georg connected various schools of group work with each other in his curriculum for "the German Way of Groupwork."

Georg was a pragmatist and above all, he loved groups and moving in the middle of people. He co-edited and co-published the book "Werkbuch für das Arbeiten mit Gruppen"1. This publication combines several contributions of different authors on the method and history, the theory and practice of social group work. The special merit of Georg on the one hand, is the further development of the theory of group phases to a circular understanding of the background of the autopoiesis of groups as living or social systems and on the other hand a remarkable compilation of resource-oriented, methodical interventions in groups. In many ways, this book is a special treasure for every group worker.

In 2008, at the annual International IASWG symposium in Cologne, Georg was named IASWG Honouree and in 2017 he received the German IASWG Badge of Honour. In 1993, Georg was one of the founders of the German chapter of the IASWG. He served on the board until 2000 and in this role, he brought his experience and knowledge into the chapter.

Until the end, he constructively contributed to the German chapter. He was instrumental in developing the chapter into a professional association, the most obvious expression of which is the certification of group workers. Georg's professional attitude, characterized by love and passion, his love for "controversy and irritation," his clear and far-sighted views and his typical and wonderful humour will be missed very much.

We mourn over the loss of our Georg. He lives on in our hearts.

Georg Nebel, Bernd Woltmann-Zingsheim (Editors.) (1997) *Werkbuch für das Arbeiten mit Gruppen.* Aachen: Verlag Heinz Kersting.

Poem

Christele wrote the poem about her experience as one of the 56 international student volunteers at the 40th International Symposium of the International Association for Social Work with Groups, Skukuza, Kruger National Park, South Africa, June 7–10, 2018.

Ubuntu means ...

Kindred hearts strung together
by the mouth of the wine bottles passed around.
Bubbles of laughter like champagne
make the bitter taste of tears palpable
as each question bares more of each person to the circle of love among us.

Dialects that are spoken through glances
while words fly around carelessly.
Encouragements poured out in high spirits without consideration of language or colour.

This is what Ubuntu means to me.
It means a hostel room that turned into a melting pot of loud nations at 2 am under a diamond-studded African sky.
It means the dizzy giggles of wine bottles clinking against teeth and the floor and against our hearts as we swallow the same pain in different flavours.
It means strength found in shared experiences no matter the continent they beat us up in and the open floor we created for us to dance into being better versions of ourselves.

Ubuntu means social worker to me.

Christele Stacey Lloyd
South African Student Volunteer)

Personal Account of the International Association of Social Work with Groups (IASWG) Symposium, Kruger National Park, South Africa

Paul Johnson

Introduction

The 2018 IASWG Symposium was held in the Kruger National Park in South Africa. This was the first time the Symposium had been held outside of North America. I recall attending the 2017 membership meeting at New York University on a hot sticky evening and Reineth Prinsloo getting up and announcing that in 2018 the Symposium would be held in South Africa in the Kruger National Park. She promised it would be a symposium we would never forget! Well, she was not kidding!

I really do not know where to begin with the superlatives to describe just how wonderful the whole experience was. For me, the journey was amazing, everything just worked like clockwork–the bus from Portland, Maine to Boston Logan Airport, the flight from Logan to Amsterdam–hey, I even had a priest sitting next to me. Now, if that was not a good sign!

When I arrived in Amsterdam, I bumped into Anna Noska and Kyle McGee and that made me feel a little more confident. Then things got even better because I ended up having three seats to myself for the ten-hour flight to Johannesburg. I guess the polite thing would have been to have gone and found Anna and Kyle, but three seats to myself, sorry that was not going to happen.

Arrival in South Africa

In Johannesburg, Anna and I walked to immigration together. Again, I was very appreciative of her company as the airport terminal signs were a little confusing. However, I had decided to stay at the Aero Lodge which was a short drive from the airport. Anna had arranged to stay at the airport hotel for the night. Yet again, just as the e-mail had instructed, I called the number for the hotel and within ten minutes there was my ride. I must admit that where I was being taken, I had no idea. The lodge was in a gated community and by the time I arrived everything was closed. A gentleman showed me to my bungalow, and I had somewhere comfortable to sleep for the night.

The next morning, I found the dining room and sat next to the wood-burning stove. A lady came in and she remarked how chilly it was. So, I invited her to join me at the table next to the fire. Well, this was another wonderful opportunity. She informed me that she was retired and lived in Alaska; however, she was in South Africa working for a veterinarian group who dispensed medications to landowners for their animals. She would be undertaking this work for the next several weeks, living in tents and travelling hundreds of miles. She also informed me that she had visited Maine and thought it to be a beautiful state.

Journey to Kruger

Now, all of this had transpired over 36 hours and I had not even arrived at Kruger yet, but before I got to my destination, I had another wonderful group work experience. Ten of us had arranged through Just Transfers to take a van from Johannesburg to Kruger. The plan was for us to meet at the information desk in the International Arrivals Terminal. Once again, everyone was on time. No one's flight had been delayed, no one had missed a connection, so the merry, but somewhat jet-lagged, band of group work travelers all boarded the van for Kruger. If my memory serves me correctly, the group included the following: Lorrie, Peter, Joan, Emily, Anne, Emma, Mamadou, Greg and Lisa.

I should at this point apologize to my fellow travelers due to the fact that I had arrived the night before and managed to get some sleep at my hotel, but for those who had just arrived and had been on flights for approximately fifteen hours, they all looked extremely tired. However, I was extremely perky and keen to make conversation. Peter, to his great credit, indulged me in polite conversation, but for the others my chatter must have been extremely annoying.

That aside, what was so wonderful about the journey to Kruger by van was the opportunity it gave us to see the country. As we left the city, we got to see some of the places where people lived. There was a stark contrast in that some of the homes looked like metal shacks, while in other places there were brick homes that were not yet completed. At the other extreme we passed homes that were extremely grand.

Another thing that I noticed was the difference in stores and people selling goods. Some of the towns we passed through had strip malls and a multitude of stores. In other places along the way, there would be just a brick building by the side of the road, which had a painted sign on it which said: "Haircuts." Another part of the journey there were people selling fruit and goods at the side of the road.

As we drove further north, the terrain changed. It became much more mountainous and we could see what appeared to be forest fires in the distance. Our journey took us through numerous small towns, past large orange groves, and what appeared to be vast forests of pine trees. Another sight that stuck with me was the color of the sky. It was just this bright blue sky. In the States during the winter, the sky is grey and extremely cloudy, but here it was extremely bright.

At around 3.30 p.m. we arrived at Kruger National Park. After completing some necessary paperwork, we could enter. It was like being on a school bus. As soon as we drove into Kruger, we saw an elephant, some zebras, a couple of giraffes, buffalo, impalas, baboons and vervet monkeys. There were lots of oooh's and awww's. "Look over here!" "Stop the bus!" Cell phones and cameras taking pictures - to say that we were all excited would be an understatement!

Welcome

We then were driven to the conference center, where, once again, much to my amazement we were greeted by Reineth and it appeared her entire family. She was hugging people, thanking them for coming, saying over and over "welcome," "welcome." Again, this was a recurring theme through the time of the Symposium. Everyone was so friendly, happy, engaging, and genuinely concerned about each other. At the reception desk, the staff could not have been more helpful. "Welcome to Kruger, your bungalow is Number 106, please take a map, and please let us know if there is anything that we can help you with."

Catching up with Friends

The other wonderful aspect of attending the IASWG Symposium is catching up with friends, and I had not been in the place five minutes and already the conversations had started. I must admit I am extremely drawn to and fond of my Irish contingent. Hence, within an hour of arriving, I was sitting on their porch, drinking wine, numerous cups of tea, catching up on family news, telling stories, and laughing so much. I was having so much fun that I did not realize the time, which frequently happens when I visit family in Ireland. I call it Irish time. It is as if all the constraints of the clock go out of the window. No one seems concerned about the actual time; they are much more focused on the moment.

Visit to After School Community Program

On Thursday two busloads of us went to two community centers: The Amukelani Center and the Siyakhula Center. It was my understanding that these two programs provide daily meals to over 100 children after school. I really do not know where to begin to describe how wonderful this visit was, but I must give credit to some of the following folks who were at the Amukelani Center. Firstly, the student volunteers who were attending the Symposium. The way they played and engaged with the children. The face painting that they did, oh my goodness!! Then there was the gentleman who came with a drum set, including a bass drum.

There were all these children sitting on the ground, with sticks and plastic paint cans following his every drum beat and playing along. It was just spectacular!

We were there for only an afternoon's visit. Yet, each day there are several volunteers who cook a meal for the children to have each day. According to the director of the program, this is the only meal the children get. Many of them are living with older siblings or are taking care of younger brothers and sisters themselves. While our visit was a fun-filled afternoon, I could not help wondering what life must be like daily for so many of these children.

Boma Braai Dinner & Informal Gathering

On Thursday evening, I attended the Boma Braai Dinner and, my goodness, the food was wonderful. Even more impressive was the number of people in attendance. As I already alluded to, I was in the company of my Irish contingent, hence, we were on Irish time so a couple of the staff helped me move a large table and we were able to join everyone. What was even more noticeable was that it appeared that there were games of musical chairs going on. People kept getting up and going over to different tables. People were hugging one another, kissing one another; there was a great deal of chatter and, more importantly, laughter. It was just a wonderful fun evening.

The Symposium

On Friday morning the "formal" Symposium commenced. Once again, we were treated to the singing and dancing of the Giyani Society for the Aged Choir. What a spectacular performance they put on for everyone. Usually you go to an opening breakfast reception and there are polite and extremely formal events, but this was loud, colorful, and invigorating. The cameras and phones were out recording the event. If you were half asleep when you walked in, you were wide awake when the choir started singing and dancing. The other wonderful aspect was the breakfast. It was a full English cooked breakfast! For the boy who grew up in the UK and often dreams of this meal, life does not get much better. They even had real tea!

By now I am sure that many of you are starting to observe some recurring themes. These being: excellent food, great company, lots of conversations, and a great deal of laughter. I should also point out that every session that I attended was very well attended. The presentations were wonderful, and, at the end of every session, each presenter was given a small gift as a thank you for their presentation.

Another noticeable issue was the number of students who were in attendance. For me, students really make the symposium. Students bring to the event so much vitality and excitement. Their importance was further illustrated to me on numerous occasions during the Symposium. Firstly, during the community visit it was the students who were doing the face painting and playing soccer and frisbee with the children. After my own presentation, a number of students came up to me and thanked me. Also, during the Symposium it was the students who were so helpful. If you went up to the information desk, they were always willing to assist you or answer a question. On one occasion one student said: "Let me take you there."

Saturday Night Game Drive & Bush Braai Dinner

Following the two days of plenary sessions, workshops, poster presentations, membership meetings, and board meetings, it was time for the Game Drive. Oh, my goodness! We all boarded the numerous buses that had been arranged for us. Little did I realize the spectacle that was about to occur – elephants, giraffes, zebras, baboons, and impalas. Elephants so close either right in front of you or right by the side of the bus, it was just unbelievable. I realized that although I had seen these animals at London Zoo as a child, seeing them in their natural habitat was just amazing. I really could not get over the size of the elephants. Despite their size they walked methodically. As for the giraffes, they were just so graceful in their movements. The fact that you could see them above the tops of the tree line was incredible.

Following the Game Drive was the Bush Braai Dinner and if Thursday's informal dinner was great, this was just out of this world. At this event I had the good fortune to sit with Dave Ward, his wife, Anne, and Jennie Fleming, the editor of *Group Work*. Now, I knew Dave from hearing his voice during several Group Work editorial board meetings. But this was the first time I had met him in person, and I found out that Dave is a huge football fan and supports Plymouth Argyle. Now anytime I find someone who can talk about football, especially about teams in the lower echelons of the English Football League, I am happy.

So there we were talking about Plymouth Argyle, Southend United, Exeter City's and Colchester United's of this world. And I informed Dave that in 1969, I had seen Watford beat Plymouth Argyle at Vicarage Road and get promoted to the old Division 2 of the football league. The other scary thing was that I could still remember the names of some of the players; but, at the same time we were being served this amazing food – beef, lamb, chicken, and a rice dish to die for. There was also wine on the table. They then announced that we could go and get dessert. Oh, my goodness, there was this warm custard over a sponge treacle pudding. Well Dave and I were like a couple of naughty schoolboys. Could we go and get more we asked?

Outdoor Experiential Session

The next day was the outdoor experiential session. While the night before I had reminisced about Southend and Plymouth, at this event I got to play football, well, kind of. The folks who worked and lived at Kruger had challenged us to a game of footy. At first, there were all these little kids on the pitch. Ok, I thought, I can give this a go. But then they miraculously disappeared, and all these big fellas showed up who were half my age and had soccer boots and the rest of the football attire.

It was not too bad of a drubbing, only three-nil; but, once again I had such a great time. In my little brain, I was 14 or 15 years of age pretending I was George Best. Only problem was that I infrequently had the ball and spent most of the time chasing these big fellas around the pitch. For about forty-five minutes it was a lot of fun.

We also had a tug of war tournament between the staff and Symposium participants. I will not tell you what the outcome of that was. All I will say is that instead of going backwards we went forwards. Following these two events there was a closing ceremony which was very touching. Again, the impetus for this was the students who had been working at the Symposium. One of them read a beautiful poem dedicated to Reineth. I do hope someone has a copy of it. Maybe it could get published in *Group Work* or in the proceedings of the Symposium.

Sunday Afternoon Walking Safari

After our athletic events morning, I went on a walking safari with a few of the folks I had driven to Kruger with from Johannesburg. I do not know if they were getting their own back on me or have one extra seat for the journey back to Johannesburg, but our two guides were at the front of the group with guns, and I somehow ended up at the back of the group. None of them seemed to be concerned either. It was a wonderful late afternoon walk, the highlight being when we spotted a Rhino. Just incredible! The other highlight of the afternoon was walking back to the van and watching that sun go down so quickly. Literally, one minute it was there and the next it was gone. Driving back, to the conference center, I could not believe how fortunate I had been to get to experience this whole adventure.

Drive back to Johannesburg

The next morning it was time for me and my fellow group of Just Transfers to head back to Johannesburg International Airport. But Kruger still had one last treat for us. Just as we were nearing the gate, we spotted a giraffe. What a sight, just so majestic in the way he walked as if there was nothing to worry about. One minute he was there and the next he was gone.

During the drive back I sat in the front with our driver, Ian, and peppered him with numerous questions, especially about sports—rugby, football, and cricket. As my wife often says about me: "Anything with a ball and he is hooked." We passed several sports stadiums and Ian informed me that the 2010 World Cup had been staged at this venue.

The journey back was as spectacular as the drive to Kruger. Again, I could not get over how blue the sky was. We passed through all the same towns again, but this time I could not help noticing as we were driving south the people that were working in many of the fields or operating stores at the side of the road were wearing jumpers or coats. I had to keep reminding myself that this was winter here in South Africa.

Before I knew it, we were pulling into the airport and then each of us was grabbing our bags and saying our goodbyes as we headed off to different airlines for our respective journeys. One minute we were all together as a group and then we were 12 individuals all with our own agendas.

Conclusion

I think I have made it abundantly clear throughout this paper that the Symposium in South Africa was wonderful. On further reflection, I wanted to try and identify what made it so outstanding. When I gave the subject some thought, the following came to mind.

Firstly, there was palatable energy and enthusiasm from the folks who were running the Symposium. Every time you saw one of them or had a question you were met with: "How can I help you?" or "What can I do for you." Nothing was too much trouble. The other thing was that outwardly they made it look effortless. Everything was under control. Secondly, the location, Kruger National Park was amazing. It was just spectacular. Also, the staff there were so helpful and friendly, and the food, oh my goodness! At the Thursday night Boma Braai Dinner and the Bush Braai Dinner, everything was prepared. It was like being in a Harry Potter movie in the dining room at Hogwarts. Everything just miraculously appeared. Yet, I am sure they did not just wave a magic wand and it was all done.

Thirdly, there were attendees. Everyone I met was so caught up in the experience; they were completely in the moment. Everywhere I went I saw people having conversations, hanging out over a cup of coffee or tea, laughing, and eating together. One lunchtime I sat outside with a lady and we ate together. We were talking away and she was telling me where she was from, where she lived, and I also told her my story. But then she said: "You know, less than thirty years ago, we could not have sat together having lunch." I can still recall watching on television in 1990 the day Nelson Mandela was released from prison.

As I have already alluded to in this paper, another group that I believe brought a great deal of energy and vitality to the Symposium were the number of students in attendance from so many schools and also from many different countries. I was so impressed on the Thursday during our community visit with how so many of the students interacted with the children. It was just outstanding.

Finally, I must return to Reineth Prinsloo. I do have to thank her for pulling this outstanding event together. I cannot imagine the countless hours she must have put into this–the phone call, emails, meetings, etc., It was truly an amazing experience. I will always remember my visit to Kruger National Park in South Africa.

Thank you!

Build the Social Justice Bridge: Participatory photography with the international group work community

Lorrie Greenhouse Gardella
and Reineth Prinsloo

Introduction

How do international social workers understand the relationship between group work and social justice? "Build the Social Justice Bridge" was a participatory photography project that engaged international group workers in an assessment of group work as a social justice profession.

The project began with the 2018 Symposium of the International Association for Social Work with Groups (IASWG), which was held in Kruger National Park, South Africa. In preparing for the symposium, we invited social workers from around the world to submit photographs and brief narratives that represented the symposium theme: "Bridging the Divide: Group Work and Social Justice." The photographs were exhibited during the opening session of the symposium, where participants reflected on their meaning for the group work community. In viewing and analyzing the photos, symposium participants identified a common vision of social justice as well as culturally specific contexts for group work, and they called for the internationalization of professional knowledge. Group work may realize its promise as a social justice profession by reaching beyond Western paradigms for research, education, and practice.

What do we mean by social justice?

Social justice is a central value and principle of the social work profession (CASW, 2005; CSWE, 2015; IFSW/IASSW, 2014; IFSW, 2018; NASW, 2017). As defined in the Global Social Work Statement of Ethical Principles (IFSW, 2018), the promotion of social justice involves challenging discrimination and institutional oppression, respecting diversity, providing access to equitable resources, resisting unjust policies and practices, and building solidarity (IFSW, 2018).

According to Harriet Goodman, "Social group workers historically recognized the power of groups as vehicles for internal change and for community action to address problems" (Goodman, 2009, p. 31). With roots in the settlement house movements of the late 19th and early 20th centuries, group work in Great Britain, North America, and Western Europe sought to prepare people living in poverty, immigrants, and other marginalized populations for citizenship in a democracy (Coyle, 1935; Coyle, 1947; Garland, Jones, & Kolodny, 1965; Kendall, 2000; Klein, 1953; Lindeman, 1980; Lowy, 1976). Group work encouraged and empowered disenfranchised communities for economic, social, and political participation (Breton, 1989; Gitterman, 2010; Gutiérrez, 1990; Lee, 2001). In a review of group work history in the United States, Albert Alissi found that through the mid-twentieth century, group workers practised in agencies, camps, neighborhood associations, and social clubs. These settings promoted the "group work ideals" of "voluntarism, mutual aid, democratic group participation, group self-government, creative program activities, advocacy, and social action" (Alissi, 2009, p. 12; Nadel & Scher, 2019; Sullivan, Mesbur & Lang, 2009). Beginning in the 1980's, when North American group work was shifting from community-based agencies to clinical settings, some researchers feared the loss of group work as a distinctive social work and social justice method (Birnbaum & Auerbach, 1994; Goodman, 2009; Simon & Kilbane, 2014; Simon & Webster, 2009).

Group workers today pursue social justice within groups, through the relationships among group members, as well as outside of groups, through social and political advocacy in the external environment (Garvin & Ortega, 2016; Ortega, 2017). The cultural context may influence whether group workers emphasize internal or external social justice issues. According to Rebecca Smith, Justin Bucchio, and Barbara Turnage (2017), group workers in the individualistic societies of the industrial West tend to focus on small group interventions, such as task groups and process groups, while group workers in the more traditional or communitarian societies of the global South tend to identify group work with larger social and political movements (Smith, Bucchio, & Turnage, 2017, p. 45).

In South Africa, as Leila Patel explains, indigenous systems of social care that once relied on social groups and cooperative practices were disrupted by colonial rule (Patel, 2015). Under apartheid, the government provided formal social welfare programs for whites only (Govender, 2016; Hölscher & Bozalek, 2012; Patel, Kaseke, & Midgley, 2012). The legacy of apartheid persists to this day, and despite demographic reforms, South Africa remains one of the most unequal societies in the world (Gandhi, 2018). In this context, South African group workers draw upon traditional communitarian values while promoting community development, political activism, and the protection of universal human rights (Midgley, 2013).

Practicing in such different environments, group workers throughout the world may be guided by social justice principles, but do they approach social justice in the same way? Is the meaning of social justice for small therapeutic groups in the U.S. so implicit as to disappear? Are group processes in South African community action programs a secondary concern? The 2018 IASWG Symposium in South Africa provided opportunities for international group workers to appreciate the culturally-specific contexts for group work, to learn from our common and different approaches to social justice, and to strengthen group work everywhere as a social justice profession.

Participatory photography as a community assessment tool

In preparing for the IASWG symposium, we faced the group work challenges of facilitating multilingual, multicultural communications and reaching beyond generalized consensus to reveal different points of view. Inspired by the methodology of photovoice (Wang & Burris, 1997), we used participatory photography as a means for entering a community assessment process.

Photovoice is a participatory research method that promotes "the ethical use of photography for positive social change" (Photovoice.

org, 2019). Guided by principles of participatory action research (PAR) and community-based participatory research (CBPR), photovoice "builds upon a commitment to social and intellectual change through community members' critical production and analysis of the visual image" (Wang, 2003, p. 181; Liebenberg, 2018; Mayfield-Johnson and Butler, 2017; Nykiforuk, Valliantaos, and Nieuwendyk, 2011; Sutton-Brown, 2014).

Caroline Wang and Mary Ann Burris introduced photovoice in 1997 as a means for understanding public health issues from the perspectives of rural Chinese women (Wang & Burris, 1997; Wang, 2003). Supported by the Ford Foundation's Yunnan Women's Reproductive Health and Development Program, the photovoice process enabled women to take and share photographs of their everyday lives. Participatory photography gave women the means for recording "community strengths and concerns," engaging in critical reflection and dialogue, and communicating with policymakers (Wang & Burris, 1997, p. 369). The photovoice process was grounded in the critical pedagogy of Paulo Friere (1973), which called for continuous listening, dialogue, and action; feminist theory, which identified the personal as political (Weiler, 1988); and documentary photography, which demonstrated the power of images as catalysts for social change (Hurley, 1972).

As Wang and Burris predicted, photovoice proved to be a "highly flexible" tool for participatory needs assessment in communities throughout the world (Wang & Burris, 1997, p. 370). In more than 20 years since the original study, photovoice has been adapted by researchers in health, education, and social science disciplines to raise awareness, agency, and self-advocacy among a wide range of communities and marginalized populations (ICR, 2019; Molloy, 2007; Photovoice.org, 2019). Some researchers, such as Linda Liebenberg (2018) and Kathleen Sitter (2017), have questioned the rigor of photovoice as a continuously evolving participatory research method. Nonetheless, photovoice has been evaluated as an effective approach for engaging with social justice issues in multicultural educational settings (Broomfield & Capous-Desyllas, 2017; Cornell & Kessi, 2017).

With "Build the Social Justice Bridge," we used a participatory photography process that adapted principles of photovoice to an assessment of the international group work community. The project shared the three basic goals of photovoice research: 1) to "enable people to identify, represent, and enhance their community" through participatory photography; 2) to "promote critical dialogue and knowledge through large and small group discussions;" and 3) to "reach policymakers," who in this case were members and leaders of IASWG (Wang & Burris, 1997, p. 369; Wang, 2003, p. 185).

We followed photovoice methodology to the extent it was possible by purposefully recruiting photographers (through IASWG); providing for the ethical use of photography (through IRB approval); proposing an initial theme for photographs ("How does group work promote social justice?"); selecting pictures to be exhibited (all submissions would be exhibited); reflecting on images through group discussions (at the IASWG Symposium session); reaching a target audience (IASWG Symposium participants); and entering a reiterative process of critical reflection, dialogue, and action (with a follow-up session at the 2019 IASWG Symposium) (Nyiforuk, Vallianatos, & Nieuwendyk, 2011; Sutton-Brown, 2014; University of Kansas, 2016; Wang, 2003).

Although inspired by photovoice, our community assessment process differed from the photovoice methodology in two significant respects (Wang & Burris, 1997; Wang, 1999). First, the subject of our community assessment, the international group work community, was a relatively privileged community rather than a marginalized population. Group workers, including students, enjoy the privileges associated with professional status. Secondly, our contributing photographers were members of an international rather than a local community, and we did not expect them to come together personally to discuss their work. Those who attended the IASWG Symposium would join directly in small group discussions, but others would be represented by proxies from their countries or universities. Considering these differences, we considered our use of participatory photography to be inspired by but distinct from the photovoice research method.

The call for photos

In February 2018, we issued an international call for photos to social work students with an interest in group work. Using the purposive and convenient sampling that is typical of photovoice (Nykiforuk, Vallianatos, & Nieuwendyk, 2011; Sutton-Brown, 2014), we posted the call for photos on the IASWG website and emailed it to IASWG members with requests that they spread the word. Submissions were to consist of: 1) a photograph or image that represents how group work promotes social justice; 2) a brief narrative of up to 50 words, 3) basic demographic information about the photographer; 4) a publication release form signed by the photographer, and 5) informed consent and publication release forms signed by any persons whose identifiable images were shown. Materials were to be sent as email attachments to the address provided. All submissions that met these criteria would be displayed at the 2018 IASWG symposium as a part of the "Build the Social Justice Bridge" symposium session.

We initially directed the call for photographs to social work students, the newest group workers, whose emerging understanding, and commitment to social justice will shape the future of the profession. Students, we believed, are well-positioned to view the current state of social work education and practice. At a time when they are reconciling classroom theories with the realities of field practice, students face unjust policies and living conditions that they may never have seen before. We hoped that participatory photography would engage students, encourage their activism, and give them a sense of agency as members of the international group work community. We later extended the call to group work educators and practitioners to expand international participation.

Screening the photos

Between February and April 2018, we received 51 photographs from 36 individual photographers who came from five countries: South Africa (16 photos); the United States (14), Germany (6), Israel (1), and the United Kingdom (1). Consistent with the photovoice community assessment process, we intended to use the photographs and narratives as starting points for a community conversation rather than as replicable data for social research (Wang, 2003). We screened submissions as we received them to confirm that the photographs and accompanying narratives related to the topic of group work and social justice.

In our admittedly subjective reviews, nearly all the photos reflected one or more of Albert Alissi's ideals of social group work (Alissi, 2009, p. 12) – voluntarism, mutual aid, democratic group participation, self-government, creative program activities, advocacy, and social action. Nearly all the photos depicted one or more of the dimensions of social justice as defined in the Global Social Work Statement of Ethical Principles (IFSW, 2018) – challenging discrimination and institutional oppression, respecting diversity, providing access to equitable resources, resisting unjust policies and practices, and building solidarity.

We soon discovered the difficulties of coding visual images and the limitations of categorizing the pictures by subjects or themes. "People with cameras can record settings as well as moments and ideas," as Wang and Burris explained (1997, p. 372), and the photographs that we received portrayed the culturally specific contexts for group work practice. Photographs of children's activity groups (evoking such themes as voluntarism, mutual aid, creative program activities, providing access) ranged from an arts and crafts group for young teens in the U.S. to a South African Christmas party for orphans with HIV. Photos of educational advocacy groups (evoking such themes as democratic participation, social action, and advocacy, resisting unjust policies) ranged from eight mothers in New York City to a large public demonstration in Pretoria. In two remarkably similar pictures, young adults were gathered in a circle as they deliberated on the papers in front of them (democratic participation, self-government, building solidarity), but these groups were worlds apart, with one group sitting on chairs in a high tech classroom and the other squatting on an earthen floor.

When we sorted the photographs by country, we found that photos from South Africa, where group work is aligned with community practice, were more likely than photos from other countries to focus on specific social justice issues, such as LGBTQ+ rights or environmental justice. On the other hand, nearly identical pictures from South Africa and the U.S. showed community gardens as the settings for group work practice. Participants in the IASWG Symposium would view all the photographs, reflect on regional similarities and differences, and consider implications for the international group work community.

The Symposium session

"Build the Social Justice Bridge," the opening session of the 2018 IASWG Symposium, brought together more than 200 group workers, including students, educators, and practitioners, from ten countries: Canada, Germany, Israel, Namibia, the Netherlands, the Republic of Ireland, South Africa, the United Kingdom, the United States, and Zimbabwe. Service users were represented by 30 members of the local Giyani Society for the Aged Choir, who welcomed the symposium with a performance and then remained to participate in the session.

The "social justice bridge" in the title of the session was not only a reference to the symposium theme but also a physical art installation – a wooden bridge at the entrance to the conference center. Participants entered the symposium by crossing over "the social justice bridge." They enjoyed a breakfast buffet and then gathered around tables in groups of about eight persons. Multilingual participants interpreted informally for those with limited English, and social work students assisted members of the choir.

After introducing the participatory photography process, we exhibited the photographs in a PowerPoint presentation that played continuously throughout the session. Also, each table was provided with prints of the photos for closer review. The small groups were invited to consider how the photos portrayed group work, social justice, and the relationship between group work and social justice; and to record their impressions on large sheets of newsprint, which we collected at the end of the session. Although representatives from the small groups reported briefly to the larger group, we did not have enough time for a large group discussion. In concluding the session, we thanked participants and encouraged them to continue the dialogue in a follow-up session at the 2019 IASWG Symposium and through their local chapter activities.

Community assessment: What did we see?

In the months following the symposium, we reviewed the written notes from the small group discussions and coded them for common themes. Concepts that were explored by all or most groups included empathy, education, history, equality, diversity, inclusion, giving voice, and intentional action. Most groups considered the South African worldview of Ubuntu or unity and oneness that has been translated as: "I am because we are" (Mugumbate & Nyanguru, 2013, p. 82). The themes that arose out of the small group discussions encompassed and expanded on Alissi's group work ideals (2009) and IFSW social justice principles (2018), as illustrated in Table 1.

Table 1: Related themes

Small-group discussions	Group work ideals (Alissi, 2009)	Social justice principles (IFSW, 2018)
Ubuntu: We need each other to make a difference Otwa Hangana: We are united The Elephant Is Ours	Voluntarism	Build solidarity
Integration of group work and social justice: Group work can turn into social justice People come together to work for social justice	Mutual aid	Build solidarity
Empathy: All pictures show empathy Use empathy, respect, acceptance, compassion	Mutual aid	Build solidarity
Inclusion: Eradicate isolation Justice comes from inclusion Oneness in groups offers strength, courage, and various solutions	Democratic participation	Build solidarity
History: Groups can overcome history Learn history and educate about skills for change	Democratic participation	Challenge discrimination and oppression
Education: Education for all is surely a bridge to justice Provide a social justice framework in education	Democratic self-government	Challenge discrimination and oppression

Empowerment: The transformative power of group experience Build support and empowerment The coming together of marginalized groups	Democratic self-government	Equitable access
Equality: Social justice is viewed as equality Bring people into equality Balance resources for the vulnerable	Democratic self-government	Equitable access
Giving Voice: Hear the voiceless Telling our stories, being heard as we intended We form bonds without words	Creative program activities	Respect diversity
Diversity: Common focus, different perspectives Connect with people different from ourselves People of different backgrounds come together to take action	Advocacy and social action	Respect diversity
Intentional action: Intention is an important ingredient Help group workers think about intentions Witness social injustice and turn it into action	Advocacy and social action	Challenge unjust policies and practices

Viewing the photos through the lens of "experiential knowledge" (Photovoice, 2018; Sutton-Brown, 2014; Wang & Burris, 1997), the small groups discussed group work and social justice as integrated processes: "Groups turn into social justice"; "People come together as a group to work on social justice issues." The small groups identified empathy as the basis for all group activities: "All pictures show empathy"; "Use empathy, respect, acceptance, and compassion." Similarly, the concept of inclusion applied to the process and purpose of group work: "Eradicate isolation"; "Justice comes from inclusion";

"Oneness in groups offers strength, courage, and various solutions."

Historical South African photographs from the anti-apartheid era led groups to consider history and the possibilities for change: "Groups can overcome history"; "Learn history and educate about skills for change." Consistent with the teachings of Paulo Friere (1973, 1974), many small groups identified education as a means and end in group work: "Education for all is surely a bridge to social justice." Education leads to empowerment, "the transformative power of the group experience."

Many groups defined social justice as equality: "Social justice is viewed as equality"; "Bring people into equality"; "Balance resources with equality for the vulnerable." Equality in education was specified as a social justice goal.

As interpreted by the small groups, the photographs illustrated the concept of giving voice: "Telling our stories in our own words and being heard as we intended"; "We can form bonds without words." Giving voice makes it possible for groups to draw on their diversity, to learn from "a multitude of perspectives and vantage points." The small groups discussed diversity not only as a value to be respected, as in the IFSW definition of social justice (2018), but also as a resource to be harnessed: "Work collaboratively with other cultures"; "People of different backgrounds come together to take action." In the views of symposium participants, group work leads to social justice through intentional action: "Intention is an important ingredient"; "Witness social injustice and turn it into action." Above all, the South African philosophy of Ubuntu inspired symposium participants to seek a global social justice culture for group work that arises out of the culturally specific experiences of group work practice.

A purpose of the symposium session, in the words of Caroline Wang, was "to produce and analyze visual images that build upon a commitment to social and intellectual change" (Wang, 2003, p. 181). In assessing the group work community, symposium participants called for social and intellectual change associated with the internationalization of professional knowledge. Small group discussions affirmed current efforts by IASWG to improve financial, linguistic, and geographical access to IASWG's programs and resources for international group workers, and they encouraged scholarship that reaches beyond prevailing Western paradigms for research, education, and practice.

Community assessment:
What did we miss?

As in our early efforts to categorize the photographs, our thematic analysis of notes from the small group discussions told only part of the story. Symposium participants interpreted the photos through both analysis and synthesis. In reflecting on the photos, they identified not only discrete concepts, but also the relationships among concepts. Out of 26 small groups, eight groups recorded their discussions with visual images – a flowering plant, a human figure, an idea map, or concentric circles – rather than with verbal lists. We could code the words on the flowering plant, but not the relationships among the words, as depicted in branches and stems.

Even when they recorded their discussions in words, some small groups alluded to culturally specific references that may have been lost in translation. One small group began its notes with the intriguing statement: "The elephant is ours: Let us finish it together." What did this mean and how did it relate to other themes? With a little research, we learned that "The Elephant Is Ours" is a local folktale about an elephant who is trampling a farmer's crops. The farmer must rely on help from other villages to deal with the elephant. He cannot cope alone. The story is an allegory for the philosophy of Ubuntu, "I am because we are." Might the elephant also represent social injustice? Is the principle of social justice, like the philosophy of Ubuntu, more fully expressed metaphorically or allegorically than literally or analytically?

In The Child's Concept of Story, a classic study of children's use of language, Arthur Applebee explained that "we function psychologically by building systematic representations of experience" (Applebee, 1978, p. 3). We use different kinds of language to express different types of "systematic representations." Transactional language, the language of logic and science, is used to represent objective reality. We respond to transactional language analytically and critically, by separating out and testing each idea. In contrast, artistic or poetic language, the language of visual images and stories, calls for appreciating the work as a whole and the interrelated patterns within its composition. Although it is possible to view art intellectually and to analyze it in transactional terms, we also engage with the artist's vision emotionally through our personal and social memories. Works of art evoke our subjective, inner worlds (Doel, 2017). Symposium participants viewed the photographs both as documentary evidence and as works of art, and some small groups responded in an artistic language of their own.

Conclusions

"Build the Social Justice Bridge" used participatory photography to engage the international group work community in an assessment of group work as a social justice profession. In response to an IASWG call for photos, 36 social workers submitted photographs and brief narratives that represented their views of group work and social justice. The photos were exhibited at the 2018 IASWG Symposium, where more than 200 participants from ten countries, including 30 South African service-users, reflected on the meaning of the photos for the group work community.

Symposium participants shared a common understanding of group work as a profession that is guided by the principle of social justice. In general, they discussed social justice as a value or principle, rather than as a set of specific, measurable goals. In applying principles of social justice to the international group work community, symposium participants supported initiatives to improve the accessibility of IASWG programs for group workers outside of North America. The photographs raised participants' awareness of the differences in the social, economic, and political environments for group work practice and the opportunities for learning that these differences provide. A significant finding from the symposium was the value of accepting both scientific and artistic systems of representation for communicating experiential knowledge. Symposium participants viewed the photographs both as documentary evidence and as works of art, and they discussed the photos in the objective, scientific language of academia and in the subjective, poetic language of stories. With their affirmation of internationalism, their belief in empathy and diversity as resources for social action, and their confidence in the possibilities for creating a more equitable society, symposium participants took a hopeful stance against the rise of ethnocentrism and nationalism in their home countries and throughout the world.

Acknowledgements

The authors are grateful to the contributing photographers, the participants in the 2018 IASWG Symposium, and the Giyani Society for the Aged Choir.

This chapter was first published in *Social Work with Groups*. vol. 44 13-16, , issue, pp, and is reproduced here by permission of Routledge.

References

Alissi, A. S. (2009). United States. In A. Gitterman & R. Salmon (Eds.), *Encyclopedia of Social work with groups* (pp. 6–13). New York: Routledge.

Applebee, A. N. (1978). *The child's concept of story.* Chicago: The University of Chicago Press.

Birnbaum, M. M, & Auerbach, C. (1994). Group work in graduate school education: The price of neglect. *Journal of Social Work Education, 30*(3), 325–336.

Breton, M. (1989). Liberation theology, group work, and the right of the poor and oppressed to participate in the life of the community. *Social Work with Groups, 12*(3), 5–18.

Broomfield, N. F. & Capous-Desyllas, M. (2017). Photovoice as a pedagogical tool: Exploring personal and professional values with female Muslim social work students in an intercultural classroom setting. *Journal of Teaching in Social Work, 37*(5), 493–512.

Canadian Association of Social Workers (2005). *CASW Code of Ethics.* Retrieved from https://www.casw-acts.ca/en/Code-of-Ethics

Cornell, J. & Kessi, S. (2017). Black students' experiences of transformation at a previously "white only" South African university: a photovoice study. *Ethnic and Racial Studies, 40*(11), 1882–1899.

Council on Social Work Education (2015). Educational Policy and Accreditation Standards. Retrieved from https://www.cswe.org/getattachment/Accreditation/Standards-and-Policies/2015-EPAS/2015EPASandGlossary.pdf.aspx

Coyle, G. (1935). Group work and social change. *Proceedings of the National Conference of Social Work* (pp. 393–405). Chicago: University of Chicago Press.

Coyle, G. (1947). *Group experience and democratic values.* New York: The Woman's Press.

Doel, M. (2017). *Social work in 40 objects (and more).* Lichfield, UK: Kirwin Maclean Associates.

Friere, P. (1973). *Education for critical consciousness.* New York: Continuum.

Friere, P. (1974). *Pedagogy of the oppressed.* New York: Basic Books.

Garland, J. A., Jones, H., & Kolodny, R. L. (1965). A model for stages of development in social work groups. In S. Bernstein (Ed.), *Explorations in group work* (pp. 17–71). Boston: Boston University.

Garvin, C. & Ortega, R. M. (2016). Socially just group work practice. In M. Reisch & C. Garvin (Eds.), *Social work and social justice* (pp. 166–197). New York: Oxford University Press.

Gandhi, D. (2018, April 18). *Africa focus: Figures of the Week: Labor market and inequality in South Africa.* Brookings. Retrieved from https://www.brookings.edu/blog/africa-in-focus/2018/04/18/figures-of-the-week-labor-market-and-inequality-in-south-africa/

Gitterman, A. (2010). Mutual aid: Back to basics. In D. M. Steinberg (Ed.), *Orchestrating the power of groups: Beginnings, middles and endings (Overtures, movements and finales)* (pp. 1–16). London: Whiting & Birch.

Goodman, H. (2009). Contemporary landscape. In A. Gitterman & R. Salmon (Eds.), *Encyclopedia of Social work with groups* (pp. 30–33). New York: Routledge.

Govender, J. (2016) Social justice in South Africa. *Civitas*, Porto Alegre, *16*(2), 237–258.

Gutiérrez, L. M. (1990). Working with women of color: An empowerment perspective. *Social Work, 35*(2), 149–153.

Hölscher, D. & Bozalek, V. G. (2012). Encountering the Other across the divides: Re-grounding social justice as a guiding principle for social work with refugees and other vulnerable groups, *British Journal of Social Work, 42*, 1093–1112.

Institute for Community Research (2019). Areas of work at ICR. Retrieved from https://icrweb.org/about-icr/

International Federation of Social Workers (2018). *Global social work statement of ethical principles.* Retrieved from https://www.ifsw.org/global-social-work-statement-of-ethical-principles/

Kendall, K. A. (2000). *Social work education: Its origins in Europe.* Alexandria, VA: CSWE Press.

Klein, A. F. (1953). *Democracy and the group.* New York: Morrow.

Lee, J. A. B. (2001). *The empowerment approach to social work: Building the beloved community.* New York: Columbia University Press.

Liebenberg, L. (2018). Thinking critically about Photovoice: Achieving empowerment and social change. *International Journal of Qualitative Methods, 17*, 1–9.

Lowy, L. (1976). *The function of social work in a changing society: A continuum of practice.* Boston, MA: Charles River Books.

Mayfield-Johnson, S. & Butler, J. (2017). Moving from pictures to social action: An introduction to Photovoice as a participatory action tool. *New Directions for Adult and Continuing Education, 154*, 49–49.

Midgley, J. (2013). Social development and social protection: New opportunities and Challenges. *Development Southern Africa, 30*(1), 2–12.

Molloy, J. K. (2007). Photovoice as a tool for social justice workers. *Journal of Progressive Human Services, 18*(2), 39–55.

Mugumbate, J. & Nyanguru, A. (2013). Exploring African philosophy: The value of Ubuntu in social work. *African Journal of Social Work, 3*(1), 82–100.

Nadel, M. & Scher, S. (2019). *Not just play: Summer camp and the profession of social work.* New York: Oxford University Press.

National Association of Social Workers (2017). *NASW code of ethics.* Retrieved from https://www.socialworkers.org/About/Ethics/Code-of-Ethics/Code-of-Ethics-English

Nykiforuk, C. I. J.; Vallianatos, H.; & Nieuwendyk, S. (2011). Photovoice as a method for revealing community perceptions of the built and social environment. *International Journal of Qualitative Methods, 10*(2), 103–124.

Ortega, R. M. (2017). Group work and socially just practice. In C. Garvin, L. M. Gutiérrez, & M. J. Galinsky (Eds.), *Handbook of social work with groups* (pp. 93–110). New York: The Guilford Press.

Patel, L. (2015) *Social welfare and social development (2nd ed.).* Cape Town: Oxford University Press.

Patel, L., Kaseke, E., & Midgley, J. (2012). Indigenous welfare and community-based social development: Lessons from African innovations. *Journal of Community Practice, 20*(1–2), 12–31.

Photovoice.org (2019). Vision and mission. Retrieved from https://photovoice.org/vision-and-mission/

Simon, S. R. & Kilbane, T. (2014). The current state of education in U.S. graduate schools of social work. *Social Work with Groups, 37*(3), 243–256.

Simon, S. R. & Webster, J. A. (2009). Struggle for survival. In A. Gitterman & R. Salmon (Eds.), *Encyclopedia of Social work with groups* (pp. 33–38). New York: Routledge.

Sitter, K. C. (2017). Taking a closer look at Photovoice as a participatory action research method. *Journal of Progressive Human Services, 28*(1), 36–48.

Smith, R., Bucchio, J., & Turnage, B. F. (2017). Social group work in a global context. In C. Garvin, L. M. Gutiérrez, & M. J. Galinsky (Eds.), *Handbook of social work with groups* (pp. 43–54). New York: The Guilford Press.

Sullivan, N. E.; Mesbur, E. S.; & Lang, N. C. (2009). Canada. In A. Gitterman & R. Salmon (Eds.), *Encyclopedia of Social work with groups* (pp. 1–6). New York: Routledge.

Sutton-Brown, C. A. (2014). Photovoice: A methodological guide. *Photography and Culture, 7*(2), 169–185.

University of Kansas (2016). Implementing Photovoice in your community. *Community tool box.* Retrieved from https://ctb.ku.edu/en/table-of-contents/assessment/assessing-community-needs-and-resources/photovoice/main

Wang, C. C. (1999). Photovoice: A participatory action research strategy applied to women's health. *Journal of Women's Health, 8*(2), 185–192.

Wang, C. C. & Burris, M. A. (1997). Photovoice: Concept, methodology, and use for participatory needs assessment. *Health education and behavior, 24*(3), 369–387.

Wang, C. C. (2003). Using Photovoice as a participatory assessment and issue selection tool: A case study with the homeless in Ann Arbor. In M. Minkler & N. Wallerstein (Eds.), *Community based participatory research for health* (pp. 179–196). San Francisco: Jossey-Bass.

Defying the labels:
The empowering role of group work in a poverty alleviation project

Gerna Wessels and Elmien Claassens

Introduction

Nelson Mandela once said: "Overcoming poverty is not a gesture of charity. It is an act of justice" (Make Poverty History, 2005). Social work commits to alleviate poverty (Zastrow, 2008). As affirmed by DuBois and Miley (2019:154): "Social work's ethical codes mandate that professionals promote social and economic justice." Many recipients of assistance become disheartened and powerless based on their experiences in these programmes, as they struggle to better their circumstances. Social work has the responsibility to develop strategies to empower people living in poverty to change their circumstances.

This paper will demonstrate how group work, as part of a poverty alleviation project, can be used to empower group members to access their inner strengths and challenge labels ascribed to them. This can be done by encouraging their active participation in group activities that build agency, which contrasts with their being passive recipients of assistance in a "top-down" manner.

A theoretical discussion of poverty and its far-reaching implications will be provided to emphasize the need for empowering group members. Empowerment will be defined as a process of guiding group members to access their power, and not the group worker "giving" power to group members. The premise of the paper is to delineate how group work can, and should, form an integral part of community development projects aimed at poverty alleviation. It will be argued how the group process can play a significant role in the support, education, and ultimate growth in the group, and the group members on an individual basis. The gains from this approach will be highlighted.

Views on poverty

Although the aim of this paper is not to provide an in-depth discussion of poverty, it is necessary to position oneself in terms of what poverty means in the context of the discussion to follow. Poverty is a multi-faceted societal issue and not easy to define. It can be defined in "economical" terms referring to the lack of money to provide for a minimum standard of living – not having enough money to buy food, clothes or provide shelter. Poverty can also be viewed as lacking aspects such as social belonging, information, worth, and dignity – much more than a lack of money (Lombard, 2014; Kranz, 2001). It is important to take note of the debate regarding the measurement of poverty, as the measurement of poverty becomes the determinant of the types of services seen as necessary to address poverty (Nayran & Petesch, 2007). For this paper, both views regarding poverty are acknowledged as complementary to each other.

Causes of Poverty

Poverty is a global phenomenon, as every society has poor members. Different opinions are found when exploring the causes of poverty. Some contend that the poor as a group are responsible or to blame for the causes of poverty. The "poor" is constructed as the "other," distinct from mainstream society (Hall, Leary & Greevy, 2014; Zastrow, 2008; duBois & Miley, 2019). They are described as possessing an alternate value system and displaying different behavioural patterns when compared to others. Proponents of this argument believe that people growing up in poverty also do not expect their lives to be different from those of their parents or grandparents, rendering them unmotivated to move out of poverty (Pemberton et al., 2016). In contrast with this view, Parrott and Maguinness (2017) argue that it is the absence of proper living environments and a lack of opportunities that determine people's positions in life, not their imperfections. Krumer-Nevo, Weiss-Gal and Monnickendam (2009) expand on this view and acknowledge the connection between poverty and issues such as gender, age, disability, ethnicity, and race.

Structural causes of poverty – placing the responsibility of poverty on society – are related to the unfair distribution of resources and opportunities due to factors such as political decision making, economic trends, wide-spread corruption, mass migration to cities and overpopulation (DuBois & Miley, 2019; Kranz, 2001).

Kirst-Ashman, Graft and Hull (2010) identify three factors likely to increase the risk of poverty, namely single parenthood, female-headed families, and race. This notion is supported by data provided in the United Nations Sustainable Development Goal 1 – "End Poverty in all its forms everywhere" where it is stated that one out of every ten people of the world population lives in extreme poverty (UN, 2015).

Consequences of poverty

Living in poverty impacts almost every aspect of a person's life (Engle & Black, 2008; Bezuidenhout, 2008; Kirst-Ashman, 2013; McCartan et al., 2018). These include:

Health

Poverty has a definite effect on the health of families. Due to their inability to pay for medical treatment or medicine, they may stay sick for long periods. Dental care is often seen as a luxury while insufficient antenatal care leads to high rates of infant mortality.

Education and employment

Limited education of parents is likely to limit the development of their children's language development, and parents are also less likely to read to their children. Parents – especially single mothers – who are constantly under stress due to their struggle for survival are more likely to use commands when talking to their children, without elaboration or explanations, with a higher incidence of negative communication. There is a higher school drop-out number amongst children from poor families, who are also less likely to engage in tertiary education.

Housing

Poor people often live in remote areas, with poor public transport and inadequate service delivery. There is a high possibility of overcrowding in their homes.

Criminal justice issues

Poor people often take risks to survive, which may include shoplifting, stealing, or selling drugs which bring them into conflict with the law. As they cannot pay for legal services, access to the justice system is often out of their reach.

Personal issues

A lack of confidence is often seen because of poverty. Continuous struggles to survive with little money, illness, and discrimination depletes poor people's confidence. The "poor" is often discriminated against – they are humiliated and treated with disrespect by service providers.

Parenting

Many parents find it difficult to meet the emotional and caregiving needs of their children, due to the stress related to their ongoing struggle for survival.

Stigmatization and labelling

A person's sense of self is formed by the interpretation of how others see them (Parrott & Maguinness, 2017). Rosenthal and Jacobson (1968) state: "People who experience stigma incorporate its negative connotations into their self-images" and "People have the tendency to live up to the labels assigned to them by others" (in duBois & Miley, 2019:151). For example, if a person or group of people is perceived as irresponsible, unmotivated, too lazy to work, and with an undesirable work ethic, it may lead to feelings of being "less" in relation to others. Krumer-Nevo et al. (2009) refer to Bullock (1995) who asserts that more powerful people see the "poor" through stereotypes and prejudices thereby "othering" them into an alternative group (Kirst-Ashman, 2013).

People living in poverty know what is being said about them, even if they choose to ignore it. In their reaction to these stigmatizing ideas about them, they may either refuse to accept these labels ascribed to them, or they may absorb these labels into their identity and see them as warranted which will unavoidably lead to negative feelings of self-loathing, hopelessness and worthlessness (Pemberton et al., 2016).

Poverty and social justice

Dominican Father Gustavo Gutierrez, a Peruvian theologian, posted the following statement in the October 24, 2016, edition of the Catholic News Service: "Poverty is not a misfortune, it's an injustice" (Tracy, 2016: no page). McCartan et al. (2018:3) add to this notion when they declare: "Poverty forms one of the structural layers of inequality that can negatively impact an individual or family."

From a social work perspective, a fair society is a society where all members have the same access to resources and benefits to living a dignified life. Social justice refers to the way sources are distributed (Hugman, 2013) and therefore, it is understandable that social work is concerned with the question of why some people are denied access to those rights which will allow them the opportunity to live a dignified life. Social justice is all about the availability and fair distribution of resources to everybody, irrespective of who they are, or what they have done in their lives (Potgieter, 1998; DuBois & Miley, 2019).

Human rights can assist anyone – the rich as well as the very poor – to establish the basis necessary to create a socially just world. Human right's concern with social justice can be found in its focus on the well-being of individuals within their social environments (Hugman,

2013; Kirst-Ashman, 2013). While human rights are concerned with access to "things" necessary to live a dignified life, social justice is concerned with the way those resources are distributed and links closely to a structural approach to the causation of poverty (Hugman, 2013). "Empowerment aims to achieve the social justice objectives of social work" (Payne, 2005:296).

Empowerment

"Poor people often feel powerless, trapped in a web of linked deprivations" (Nayaran et al., 2000:235) and "must be empowered to see that change is possible" (Dubois & Miley, 2019:244). Power cannot be given to people (Mullender et al., 2013), but they can be helped to gain access to power in themselves, in and with each other and the environment. It is the task of social work to empower clients living in poverty (Kirst-Ashman, 2013).

In working with a disenfranchised group of people such as people living in poverty, it is important to help them gain access to power in themselves to create their destinies and future, whereby they gain a sense of accomplishment (DuBois & Miley, 2019; Kirst-Ashman et al., 2010). To empower the women who were part of the Moola project (that will be elaborated on further in this paper), group work was specifically selected as the primary intervention. DuBois and Miley (2019:80) propose: "As a social work method, group work is an empowerment-oriented strategy for working collaboratively for change with individuals and extends its application to working with organizational and community groups." Kirst-Ashman (2013) suggests that empowerment group work should help women define their self-worth and values before attempting to improve their lives. They need to explore themselves first and only then make plans to improve their lives and environment.

Poverty alleviation

"In 2018–2019, 17.6 million beneficiaries received monthly grants in South-Africa, and it is estimated that 18.7 million beneficiaries will receive social grants in 2021/22" (RSA, 2019). Although social grants play an important role in alleviating poverty, it does not provide a permanent solution to poverty. Poverty alleviation needs to provide opportunities to exercise agency to enable people to act to effect change in their situations (Lombard, 2014).

Social work as a profession has always been committed to alleviating poverty (Zastrow, 2009) and therefore social workers will play a major role in delivering social services to the vulnerable in society. As the poor themselves know their situations and needs best, they have to be involved in any form of poverty alleviation effort (RSA, 1997; Kranz, 2001; Narayan & Petesch, 2007; Engle & Black, 2008; Pemberton, et al., 2016; Lombard, 2014). Patel emphasises in this regard: "Poverty will not be automatically reduced as the economy grows but needs to be tackled head-on with other social interventions" (Patel, 2015:112).

Bearing this in mind, an example of a poverty alleviation project, driven by the Funanani Trust, a community based non-governmental organisation delivering social work services since 1998 will be discussed. This discussion will demonstrate how group work can function as a vehicle for social development as part of a poverty alleviation project.

The Moola Project

Context

Funanani Trust is a non-government social services provider based in Mamelodi and Soshanguve in Pretoria, South Africa, areas characterized by high levels of poverty, unemployment, and inequality regarding access to services. Since its inception 22 years ago, Funanani Trust has provided a holistic approach to poverty alleviation, through its two early childhood development (ECD) centres for orphaned and vulnerable children, a youth development project preparing young people for the job market, as well as a fully functional English-medium primary school. Funanani Trust also partners with lawyers of the Law Society of the Northern Provinces of the country to render pro-bono legal services to community members thereby providing access to the justice system despite their inability to pay for these services.

The Moola project, launched as one of Funanani Trust's projects in 2016, is a unique project that seeks to address the socio-economic aspect of poverty alleviation. This project functions in the following manner: Parents/caregivers of children in the ECD centres can earn credits – so-called Moolas – which they use to "buy" items from the Moola shop according to their needs. The accumulated Moolas can then be used as a currency to purchase goods of the service user's choice according to their experienced needs and preferences, from the Moola shops set up in the two community centres.

The word "Moola" is derived from the South-African informal (slang) word "Moolah" which means money. According to the Free Dictionary (2020), Moolah means: "Something, such as coins or printed bills, used as a medium of exchange." In the context of this project, Moolas are credits to be exchanged for items of choice. The items in the Moola shop include goods such as basic food items, baby food and toiletries, cleaning materials, stationery, toys, clothes, and even furniture. Participants participate in activities to earn Moola points and these activities amongst others include volunteering at the Early Childhood Development Centre and attending group work and workshops facilitated by social work students and the Funanani care workers. Attendance of group work is an indispensable part of the broader Moola project whereby community members can earn Moolas.

Group work and poverty alleviation

As stated earlier, poverty is more than an economic injustice but also constitutes a socio-economic injustice. Through group work, participants in this poverty alleviation project are given "a voice" and provided with opportunities to use their capabilities to grow and develop. Weyers (2011) emphasises the use of task groups in empowering group members with the focus on the development of their "self-help, leadership, problem-solving and other abilities" (p. 154)." Sitepu (2014) also refers to an empowerment-driven group work programme aimed at developing the potential and strengthening the capacity of its members in a poverty alleviation programme in Indonesia. In this development programme, group work served as a vehicle for change, and a resource for developing social competencies.

By participating in group work, the "poor" can make their voices heard. They can make their own decisions, without being told what to do or being perceived as incapable of making their own decisions (Parrott & Maguinness, 2017; The World Bank Group, 2001).

Empowerment group work provides opportunities for group members to be heard – often for the first time in their lives. It also provides opportunities to build capabilities and to empower them with knowledge. "As a social work method, group work is an empowerment-oriented strategy for working collaboratively with group members" (DuBois & Miley, 2019:80; Toseland & Rivas, 2012) and provides members with a sense of social belonging, respect, and dignity. This has relevance in the context of poverty alleviation, as the poor are a marginalised group – suffering from social exclusion and stigmatisation.

Group work, as part of the Moola project, is based in a commitment to social justice and embodies the principles for working in a poverty alleviation project as stated by Mullender et al. (2013:49):

- The belief that people are experts in their own lives.
- The belief that people have the right to define themselves and not have negative labels imposed onto them.
- The right to be heard.
- The belief that individual problems can be interpreted as shared concerns and be dealt with collectively.
- The belief that collaboration between people can be powerful.
- The belief that the group facilitator is not a "leader," but an enabler aimed at supporting group members to make their own decisions and take ownership of the outcomes.

The Group Work Programme

Group members are recruited from the Moola project participants. Although group members earn Moola points for their participation, it is not a prerequisite for participation in the larger Moola project. All members are parents/caregivers of children in the Funanani ECD centres, with a wide range in age. Membership is voluntary and not a pre-requisite for participation in the Moola project. Group membership fluctuates, as members drop out when they find employment or due to personal responsibilities. New members are added to the group as they join the project. The group resembles a so-called "self-directed group" with a social worker or social work student as a facilitator, while members determine the agenda and themes of the group work sessions according to their needs (Mullender et al., 2013).

Masson et al. (2012) juxtapose leader-directed groups with group-directed groups. The authors prefer a leader-directed leadership style as they propose that group members often "do not know what they need" and see this type of leadership style as "a waste of time" (Masson et al., 2012:25). In the Moola groups, the social workers and group members take joint responsibility for the groups. Group members are perceived as experts of their own lives, therefore fully able to participate in determining the agenda for the group sessions. Sharing responsibility with group members plays a vital role in the empowerment focus of the group work. Group sessions are facilitated according to the needs of the group members.

In the Moola group, members identified varying themes to be addressed in the group work sessions. Here are some examples:

Many grandmothers use their old age grants, received as a government benefit, to take care of their grandchildren, as the mothers are unemployed or have passed away. The relationship between the grandmothers and mothers are often characterised by conflict and a lack of understanding, impacting on the well-being of the children.

- Parental skills were high on the agenda of the group members. As poverty causes stress in mothers, they find it difficult to maintain their loving relationships with their children. Mothers also shared amongst themselves how they discipline their children.
- Another important component of the group work was the position of the father in the lives of the children. Many fathers do not form part of their children's lives and the mothers suffer to a great extent to take care of the children. Issues such as the importance of the father figure were discussed in the groups. Mothers were empowered to assert themselves if they wanted to engage with the father/s of their children.
- One of the sessions that was thoroughly enjoyed by the group members was the activity-based attachment group for mothers/caregivers of young children. Mothers were empowered with skills to read or tell stories and play games with their children, irrespective of their educational level. The children participated in the group to make it a "hands-on" experience for the mothers.
- A group of young mothers participated in a computer literacy group to enhance their skills. They also prepared their CV's and applied online for potential job opportunities. Group members supported each other in the often-discouraging process of finding employment. They would meet weekly to share their experiences

and support each other.

- Another interesting group was the entrepreneurship skills group aimed at empowering members with knowledge and skills for starting small businesses. In this group, members were divided into smaller groups of four with at least one member with competency in a skill such as cooking, baking, sewing, or beading. They were challenged to start a small venture to market their business. They joined the group every week where they shared their successes and struggles and supported each other.
- Topics such as saving, budgeting, and becoming debt-free formed an important part of the group work and some opened a personal savings account.
- All groups provided opportunities for input to improve the Moola project to have their say in the way the project is run.

Discussion

Group members were highly motivated to attend the group work sessions. Not only were the task groups found to be helpful, but, so too the different treatment groups as described by Toseland and Rivas (2014), namely educational, growth, support, and socialization groups. It needs to be noted that the goal of the group work was not to provide therapy but to strengthen the group members. As the members were increasingly able to shape their future and the future of their children, their self-esteem and feelings of self-worth were raised. Perlman in Narayan and Petesch (2007:26) asserts "a sense of agency, optimism, perseverance, and aspirations significantly correlated with different measures of successful outcomes."

Through the group work, the members formed supportive relationships which played an important role in breaking the isolation often experienced by marginalized groups such as people living in poverty. As the group members met others who have struggled and found ways to assume some control over their lives, it inspired a new sense of optimism and hope in their lives. This gave members the confidence that they have the power to choose to be different (Corey et al., 2007). Empowerment counters hopelessness and powerlessness with an emphasis on the ability of each person to address problems competently, beginning with a positive view of the self (Zastrow, 2009).

Group members are living proof that people do "not deserve the negative labels which are pinned on them, but in fact, they are full of positives: they have strengths, skills, the ability to do things for themselves and much to offer one another" (Mullender et al., 2013:32). Lombard (2014) refers to the strengths of the poor as cited by The United Nations (1999:8) as "… their inherent good sense of what is most important for surviving in a difficult and unpredictable environment." Group members also reported positive changes in their capabilities in terms of parenting skills and entrepreneurial skills.

Social workers who facilitated the group work realised that they sometimes did not look beyond the labels, but if group members were provided the opportunity to contribute their ideas – if they were listened to and encouraged to act on their suggestions – they presented differently. Once treated with respect, group members become much abler than people assume.

Group members' contributions regarding the functioning of the community work project were invaluable. They provided suggestions regarding the activities they felt should qualify for Moola points, how volunteer possibilities could be expanded, and highlighted areas of concern.

Conclusion and recommendations

Social work must take up the call to serve social justice by empowering people living in poverty to access their inner capabilities to change their circumstances. The empowerment group work focused on the lived experiences of the group members, starting with the mothers themselves. Their self-confidence increased as they became aware of their personal value in their circumstances. In contrast with being passive recipients of assistance in a "top-down" manner, the group work provided group members the opportunity to challenge the labels often ascribed to them by demonstrating their motivation to participate in the programme. The group work empowered group members to make changes in their lives on their terms, and according to their own needs and strengths.

Group work is a powerful tool that helps empower people to make their voices heard and to encourage their active participation in improving their well-being.

References

Bezuidenhout, F. J. (Ed.) (2008). *A reader on selected social issues.* (4th ed.). Pretoria: Van Schaik.

Corey, M. S., Corey, G., & Corey, C. (2007). *Groups: Process and practice.* (8th ed.). California: Brooks/Cole.

DuBois, B. & Miley, K. K. (2019). *Social Work. An empowering profession.* (9th ed.). Boston: Pearson.

Engle, P. L. & Black, M. M. (2008). *The effect of poverty on child development and educational outcomes. Annals of the New York Academy of Science.* Retrieved from https://doi.org/10.1196/annals.1425.023

Government of New Brunswick Government 2014–2019 Progress Report *What is poverty?* Retrieved from https://www2.gnb.ca/content/gnb/en/departments/esic/overview/content/what_is_poverty.html

Hall, S., Leary, K., & Greevy, H. (2014). *Public attitudes to poverty.* Joseph Rowntree Foundation. Retrieved from https://www.jrf.org.uk›report›public-attitudes-towards-poverty

Hugman, R. (2013). *Culture, values and ethics in social work. Embracing diversity.* Abingdon: Routledge.

Kirst-Ashman, K. K. (2013). *Introduction to Social work and Social Welfare: Critical thinking perspectives* (4th ed.). Belmont: Brooks/Cole.

Kirst-Ashman, K. K. & Hull, G. H. Jr. (2010). *Understanding generalist practice. International Edition.* USA: Brooks/Cole.

Kranz, L. (2001). *The Sustainable Livelihood Approach to Poverty Reduction. An introduction.* Swedish International Development Cooperation Agency. Division for Policy and Socio-Economic Analysis.

Krumer-Nevo, M., Weiss-Gal, I., & Monnickendam, M. (2009). Poverty-aware social work practice: a conceptual framework for social work education. *Journal of Social Work Education, 45*(2), 225–243.

Lombard, A. (2014). Entrepreneurship in Africa: Social work challenges for human, social and economic development. *Social Work/Maatskaplike Werk, 39*(14), 224–237.

Make poverty history. (2005). Retrieved from www.mandela.gov.za/mandela_speeches/2005/050203_poverty.htm

Masson, R. L., Jacobs, E. E., Riley, L., & Schimmel, C. J. (2012). *Group counselling. Interventions and techniques.* (7th ed.) Belmont, CA: Brooks/ Cole.

McCartan, C., Morrison, A., Bunting, L., Davidson, G., & McIlroy, J. (2018). "Stripping the wallpaper of practice: Empowering social workers to tackle poverty," *Social Sciences, 7*(10), 1–16. https://doi.org/10.3390/socsci7100193

Free Dictionary. (2020). Moolah. Retrieved from www.thefreedictionary.com

Mullender, A., Ward, D., & Flemming, J. (2013). *Empowerment in Action. Self-directed groupwork.* Hampshire: Palgrave Macmillan.

Narayan, D. & Petesch, P. (Eds.) (2007). *Moving out of poverty. Cross-disciplinary perspectives on mobility. Volume one.* Washington: World Bank.

Nayaran, D., Chambers R., Skah, M., & Petesch, P. (2000). *Voices of the poor crying out for change.* New York: Oxford University Press.

Nwonwu, F. (Ed.) (2008). *The Millennium Development Goals. Achievements and prospects of meeting the targets in Africa.* Pretoria: Africa Institute of South-Africa.

Parrott, L. & Maguinness, N. (2017). *Social Work in context. Theory and concept.* Los Angeles: Sage.

Patel, L. (2015). *Social Welfare and Social Development in South Africa.* (2nd ed.). Cape Town: Oxford.

Pemberton, S., Sutton, E. J., Fahmy, E., & Bell, K. (2016). "Navigating the stigmatised identities of poverty in austere times: resisting and responding to narratives of personal failure," *Critical Social Policy, 36*(1), 21–37. doi.org/10.1177/0261018315601799

Payne, M. (2005). *Modern social work theory* (3rd ed.). London: Palgrave Macmillan.

Potgieter. M.C. (1998). *The Social Work Process. Development to empower people.* South-Africa: Prentice Hall.

R.S.A. Ministry for Welfare and Population Development. (1997). White Paper for Social Welfare. Notice 1108 of 1997. Government Gazette, 386 (18166). Pretoria, 8 August. Retrieved from http://www.polity.org. za/govdocs/white_papers/social971.html

RSA National Treasury. (2019). Estimates of National Expenditure. Retrieved from http://www.treasury.gov.za/dcuments/National%20Budget/2019/enebooklets/Vote%2017%20Social%20Development.pdf

RSA Presidency of the Republic of South Africa. National Planning Commission (2015). National development plan. Retrieved from https://nationalplanningcommission

Saleebey, D. (2009). Introduction: Power in People. In Saleebey. D. (Ed.).

The strengths perspective in Social Work Practice. (5th ed.) Boston, MA: Pearson-Allyn and Bacon.

Sitepu, A. (2014). *Role of social workers in facilitating of the poverty alleviation program in Indonesia.* The Center for Research and Development Retrieved from https://msocialwork.com/index.php/aswj/article/view/9

The World Bank Group. (2001). *Poverty Reduction and Economic Management/ Human Development/ Development Economics.* Retrieved from www2. unesco.org/wef/en-docs/findings/efastatdoc.pdf

The World Bank Group. *Chapter 2. The definitions of poverty.* Retrieved from https://siteresources.worldbank.org

Toseland, R. W. & Rivas, R. F. (2014). *An introduction to group work practice.* (7th ed.). USA: Allyn and Bacon.

Tracy, D (2016). Catholic News Service. Retrieved from http://catholicphilly. com/2016/10/news/national-news/poverty-not-a-misfortune-but-an-injustice-says-peruvian-theologian/

United Nations. (2015). *Transforming our world: The 2030 agenda for sustainable development.* Advanced unedited version. Finalised text for adoption (1 August) Retrieved from
https://sustainabledevelopment.un.org./content/documents

Weyers, M. L. (2011). *The theory and practice of community work: A Southern African perspective.* (2nd ed.). Potchefstroom: Keurkopie.

Zastrow, C. H. (2008). *Introduction to social work and social welfare. Empowering people.* (9th ed.). Belmont, CA: Brooks/Cole.

Zastrow, C. H. (2009). *Social work with groups. A comprehensive workbook.* (7th ed.). Belmont, CA: Brooks/Cole.

Gemeinwesenarbeit und Social Groupwork am Beispiel des ökumenischen Stadtteilnetzwerkes „Netzanschluss"

Ulrike Overs

Einführung

Dieser Aufsatz beschreibt die Gründung und Entwicklung eines Stadtteilnetzwerkes für alleinerziehende Eltern und ihre Kinder, das vor etwa 15 Jahren in Aachen, Deutschland, ins Leben gerufen worden ist. Initiiert worden ist dies im Aachener Westen von der katholischen und evangelischen Kirchengemeinde, die jeweils einen großen Handlungsbedarf wahrgenommen haben. Um die Motivation der Initiatoren zu verstehen, wird zunächst die Situation Alleinerziehender in Deutschland aufgezeigt; zum einen wird die Gefährdung in (relative) Armut zu geraten beschrieben, zum anderen soll deutlich gemacht werden, wie sich die Lebenssituation vieler Alleinerziehender darstellt.

Die demographische Entwicklung im Stadtviertel wird anschließend beschrieben. Informationen zum Wohnumfeld und Stadtviertel mit seiner historischen Entwicklung zu geben sowie Probleme aber auch Ressourcen des Viertels zu beschreiben, halte ich für grundlegend, um die Lebenssituation und Anliegen des Netzwerkes nachvollziehen zu können.

Das Hauptaugenmerk des Aufsatzes liegt auf der Beschreibung und Umsetzung des Stadtteilnetzwerkes. Dabei bietet die Methode des Social Groupwork die Basis der bedarfs- und prozessorientierten Arbeit unter Beteiligung aller Akteure.

Seit Gründung des Stadtteilnetzwerkes Netzanschluss ist mir seine

Entwicklung, Leitung und Koordination anvertraut worden. Beim 40. Internationalen Symposium der IASWG in Skukuza, Südafrika, durfte ich meine sozialpädagogische Arbeit vorstellen. Anhand von Berichten und Fotos habe ich den Teilnehmenden einen kleinen Einblick über diese Initiative verschafft. Diese Präsentation ist Grundlage dieses Artikels. Um die Situation alleinerziehender Eltern in Deutschland zu verdeutlichen sowie deren Situation im gesamtgesellschaftlichen Kontext sehen zu können, habe ich mein Referat entsprechend ergänzt.

[Abschließend zum Verständnis noch eine kurze Erklärung: Wenn es im Text darum geht, differenziert Männer oder Frauen zu benennen, nutze ich beispielsweise die Schreibweise: Mitarbeiter*innen stellvertretend für Mitarbeiterinnen und Mitarbeiter.]

Setting und Kontext

Pollert et al. (2016) definieren Armut als:

„…. die wirtschaftliche Situation einer Person oder Gruppe von Menschen, in der diese nicht aus eigener Kraft einen als angemessen bezeichneten Lebensunterhalt bestreiten kann (objektive Armut) oder ihre Lage selbst als Mangel empfindet (subjektive Armut). Welcher Lebensunterhalt jeweils als angemessen betrachtet wird, verändert sich mit der kulturellen, wirtschaftlichen und sozialen Situation der Gesellschaft, weshalb international von absoluter Armut (sehr niedriges pro Kopf Einkommen) und relativer Armut (im Vergleich zur Bevölkerung eines Landes) gesprochen wird. Dem Schutz vor Armut dient z.B. die Grundsicherung, mit der das wirtschaftlich-soziale Existenzminimum gesichert werden soll. In der Wirtschaftsstatistik gilt als armutsgefährdet, wer über weniger als 60 % des mittleren Einkommens der Gesamtbevölkerung verfügt."

In Anlehnung an die oben zitierte Definition spreche ich im weiteren Text, wenn nicht anders bezeichnet, von relativer Armut. Da es sich bei der Adressatengruppe des von mir beschriebenen Stadtteilnetzwerkes schwerpunktmäßig um Alleinerziehende handelt, werde ich mich bei meiner Ausführung auf diese Personengruppe beschränken.

Armut in Deutschland

Armutsrisiken

Ältere Menschen, Menschen mit Migrationshintergrund, kinderreiche Familien sowie Alleinerziehende gehören zu den Gruppen, die in Deutschland von Armut bedroht sind. Meine langjährige Erfahrung zeigt, dass alleinerziehende Eltern meist in der Situation sind, Familie und Beruf allein zu vereinbaren und unter großem Druck stehen. Untermauert werden meine Erfahrungen von der Bertelsmannstudie (Bertelsmannstudie, 2013). Mangelnde Vereinbarkeit von Familie und Beruf bringt meist eine Vielzahl von Problemen mit sich. Zahlreiche Publikationen des „Verbands Alleinerziehende Mütter und Väter" (VAMV) beschreiben das auf ihrer Internetseite. Betreuungs- und Arbeitszeiten decken sich nicht – es kann häufig nur mit reduzierter Stundenzahl erwerbstätig gearbeitet werden, was finanzielle Einbußen mit sich bringen. Viele Arbeitsbereiche erfordern Flexibilität, z.B. Reisen, Nacht- und Wochenenddienste. Dies ist ohne Betreuung der Kinder nicht zu leisten. Eine weitere Hürde besteht, wenn die Arbeitsstätte viele Kilometer vom Wohnort entfernt ist, was mehr Zeit und Fahrtkosten verursacht. Viele müssen aufgrund der oben erwähnten Problematik ihren erlernten Beruf aufgeben und nehmen häufig einen anderen schlecht bezahlten und unzureichend abgesicherten Job an, um Kinderbetreuung und Erwerbstätigkeit miteinander zu verbinden.

Ein weiteres Problem entsteht, wenn Arbeitgeber alleinerziehende Frauen nicht einstellen, aus Sorge, dass sie bei Krankheit der Kinder oder aus Gründen der Überlastung zu häufig ausfallen könnten. Diese Erfahrung machen viele Frauen des Netzwerkes. Im Austausch mit Kolleg*innen werden diese Annahmen ebenfalls benannt. Eine kürzlich veröffentliche Studie bestätigt die Erfahrungen (VAMV, 2019).

In Deutschland sind Väter verpflichtet, Unterhalt für die Kinder zu zahlen. Allerdings wird das von einem Großteil nicht geleistet beziehungsweise die Zahlungen entsprechen nicht dem, was den Kindern tatsächlich zusteht. Schwab (2016) beschreibt in ihrem Online Bericht „Warum viele Väter nicht zahlen," dass nur ein Drittel der unterhaltspflichtigen Väter regelmäßig den vollen Unterhalt für ihre Kinder zahlen, zwei Drittel zahlen zu wenig oder gar nicht. Im Idealfall übernimmt der Staat einen Unterhaltvorschuss, der jedoch vergleichbar gering ausfällt. Bittere Kämpfe und heftige Konflikte der Eltern untereinander sowie anschließende Gerichtsverfahren ziehen sich häufig über viele Jahre hinweg. Da sich die Rente an der Höhe des Einkommens orientiert, fällt diese aufgrund des geringeren Einkommens für das Elternteil, das die Familienarbeit geleistet hat, meist viel niedriger aus (VAMV, 2019).

Auswirkungen von Armut auf das Leben der Ein Eltern Familien

Aufgrund von Trennung, Scheidung oder Tod eines Elternteils ändert sich bei den meisten Familien die finanzielle Situation schlagartig; es fehlt plötzlich ein Einkommen. Eine doppelte Haushaltführung stellt eine große finanzielle Belastung dar und das betreuende Elternteil kann gegebenenfalls einer bisherigen Beschäftigung nicht mehr wie gewohnt nachgehen (vgl. VAMV, 2019).

Für diejenigen, die zugunsten der Kinderbetreuung beziehungsweise zur Unterstützung des Partners auf dem Weg zu dessen Karriere eine Zeit lang keiner bezahlten Arbeit nachgegangen sind, ist es meist schwer, im Arbeitsmarkt wieder Fuß zu fassen. Entsprechende Maßnahmen des Jobcenters versuchen dem entgegen zu wirken, was sich in ihren Integrationsprogrammen zeigt (vgl. Jobcenter Städte Region Aachen, 2018).

Familien, die ein gutes Auskommen hatten, müssen sich plötzlich stark einschränken und leben häufig an der Armutsgrenze. „Als ich noch mit meinem Mann und den Kindern zusammengelebt habe, hatten wir ein geräumiges Haus mit Garten in einem schönen Wohngebiet. Heute bin ich froh, die Miete für eine kleine Wohnung für mich und meine Kinder eigenständig stemmen zu können" (Aussage einer dreifachen Mutter aus unserem Netzwerk, 2014). Eine 45-Jährige berichtet (2017):

> *„Früher hatten wir ein offenes Haus und häufig Gäste, für die ich gerne und großzügig gekocht habe und mit denen wir bis tief in die Nacht gemütlich zusammen gesessen haben. Das ist finanziell in diesem Rahmen nicht mehr möglich, Einladungen werden seltener, „Freunde" ziehen sich zurück."*

Familien, die als 2 Eltern Familien bereits sehr finanziell eingeschränkt waren, laufen Gefahr noch weiter in Armut zu geraten.

Darüber hinaus gibt es auch Familien, die sich nach einer Trennung zwar meist einschränken müssen, jedoch trotzdem ein finanziell abgesichertes Lebens führen können.

Dank der Unterstützung durch den Staat ist die Grundsicherung armer Familien in Deutschland gegeben, wie es das Bundesministerium für Arbeit und Soziales vorgibt (vgl. Bundesministerium für Arbeit und Soziales). Allerdings handelt es sich hierbei wirklich nur um die Grundsicherung. Zahlreiche Gespräche mit Betroffenen und der Austausch mit Kolleg*innen aus Beratungseinrichtungen bestätigen meinen Eindruck und zeigen auf, dass es einer sehr guten Haushaltsführung bedarf, um mit dieser Transferleistung auszukommen. Ereignisse wie Krankheiten, medizinische Hilfsmittel (Brille, Zahnersatz ...), größere Reparaturen, Mieterhöhungen oder notwendige Anschaffungen werfen große Probleme auf. „Eigentlich ist es üblich, die Operation (Anmerkung: es handelte sich um die Entnahme eines Knochenstückes der Hüfte) mit Vollnarkosen durchzuführen. Allerdings hätte ich den Mehrpreis selbst bezahlen müssen. So habe ich mich für die örtliche Betäubung entschieden, die ich finanziert bekommen habe. Die Schwester im Operationssaal war sichtlich irritiert über meine Entscheidung." (Aussage einer vierfachen Mutter des Netzwerkes, 2013). Häufig sehen Familien sich gezwungen, sich zu verschulden, was ihre Lage zusätzlich erschwert.

Auch in Deutschland gibt es viele Familien, die sich schwertun, ihre Kinder mit ausreichend Essen zu versorgen. Essensausgaben für Bedürftige (Tafeln) haben großen Zulauf (Tafel Deutschland) Die Aussage einer dreifachen Mutter unseres Netzwerkes bestätigt das: „Seit ich mich bei foodsharing als Lebensmittelretterin engagiere, kann ich mich richtig satt essen."

Der deutsche Armutsforscher Christoph Butterwegge befasst sich seit Jahrzehnten mit der Problematik der mangelnden Teilhabe finanziell benachteiligter Menschen und beschreibt den Teufelskreis Armut (Butterwegge, 2001) bereits 2001 in einem gleichnamigen Artikel.

Auch Teilhabemöglichkeit bei kulturellen, sozialen und freizeitmäßigen Angeboten sind eingeschränkt bis nicht möglich. Die in Deutschland beschriebenen gleichen Bildungschancen für alle Kinder sind eine Illusion, da Bildung Geld kostet (Musikunterricht, Eintrittspreise in Museen und zu Veranstaltungen, Urlaubsreisen, Nachhilfe, Mitgliedsbeiträge bei Sportvereinen und so weiter (VAMV, 2019).

Mangelnde Teilhabemöglichkeit durch finanzielle Armut hat meist soziale Armut zur Folge. Mitglieder unseres Netzwerkes beschreiben, dass sie eine Einladung nicht annehmen, da das Gastgeschenk nicht finanziert werden kann oder nicht zurück eingeladen werden kann. Gemeinsame Treffen mit Freunden in Kneipen und Cafés sind nicht (mehr) möglich, viele Freizeitaktivitäten kosten Geld – da es nicht vorhanden ist, bleibt man zuhause. Wenn dieser Prozess über Jahre andauert, führt das bei vielen Menschen in die Einsamkeit.

Arm zu sein in einem reichen Land ist mit Scham besetzt. „Ich verzichte selbst eher auf Essen, ehe ich in der Schule zugeben würde, die Kosten für den Tagesausflug meines Kindes nicht zahlen zu können und um Unterstützung zu bitten." (Aussage einer Mutter der Gruppe, 2018) oder eine andere Frau (2019): „Beim Anstehen vor der Tafel ziehe ich immer die Mütze tief ins Gesicht, um unerkannt zu bleiben. Besonders schmerzhaft ist es, von Passanten beschimpft zu werden und als Sozialschmarotzer bezeichnet zu werden." Arm zu sein erfüllt viele Menschen mit Scham, da sie häufig den Eindruck haben, versagt zu haben.

Seit Jahren mache ich diese Erfahrung, die von vielen Kolleg*innen bestätigt werden. Darüber hinaus machen Frauen und Männer auch die Erfahrung als arme Menschen nicht die gleiche Wertschätzung zu erhalten wie diejenigen, denen es finanziell besser geht. Sie erleben das in Schule, Nachbarschaft und auch sehr häufig bei Mitarbeiter*innen der entsprechenden Ämter. „Als der Lehrerin klar wurde, dass wir von Transferleistungen leben, schwankte sie mit der Gymnasialempfehlung für meinen Sohn und meinte, dann sei eine Realschule sicherlich die geeignetere Schule. Ich könnte dem Kind bei auftretenden Schwierigkeiten ja nicht unterstützend zur Seite stehen. Armut wird häufig mit geringer Bildung gleichgesetzt" (Dreifache Mutter des Netzwerkes, 2012).

Finanzielle Armut kann Menschen aller sozialen Milieus treffen. Bei Fachausschusstreffen beschreiben Kolleg*innen die Erfahrung, dass die problematische finanzielle Situation „Normalverdienern" nicht bewusst ist. Dies würde ihnen immer wieder in Gesprächen mit Bekannten und Freunden bewusst. In den Medien wird nach den Erfahrungen von Maja Malik (2019) häufig sehr einseitig und wenig komplex über das Thema Armut berichtet.

Es besteht die Annahme, durch Grundsicherung wäre für alles gesorgt. Außerdem wird das „Armsein" häufig, wie oben beschrieben, so geschickt versteckt, dass dem Umfeld die wirklich problematische Situation der Familien häufig nicht bewusst ist.

Ein weiterer Aspekt der sozialen Armut ist, dass sich mit Trennung oder Scheidung auch häufig das soziale Netzwerk verändert beziehungsweise ganz wegbricht. Schwiegerfamilien und Freunde ziehen sich in vielen Fällen aus unterschiedlichen Beweggründen zurück. Aus diesem Grund schließen sich die meisten Frauen mit ihren Kindern unserem Angebot an. Sie sind, ihren Aussagen entsprechend, darauf angewiesen, sich ein neues Netzwerk aufzubauen und einen kleinen Ersatz für Familie zu suchen. Bestehende Kontakte werden häufig nach Trennungen abgebrochen oder verändern sich, da eine Scheu oder Unwohlsein besteht, als Einzelperson mit Paaren etwas gemeinsam zu unternehmen. Erzählungen machen auch deutlich, dass verheiratete Frauen sich wenig solidarisch zeigen, da sie unter anderem die Alleinerziehende als Konkurrentinnen erleben, so wie folgende Aussagen bestätigen. „Ich mag meinen Nachbarn nicht mehr bitten, mir bei kleinen handwerklichen Arbeiten zu helfen. Nach 5 Minuten wird von der Ehefrau das gemeinsame Kind geschickt, um den Vater zum Essen abzuholen. Ich vermute sie hat Sorge, dass ich ihr den Mann ausspannen möchte – ein Gedanke von dem ich weit entfernt bin!" (Mutter des Netzwerkes, 2015) und eine andere Frau (2018): „Seit mein Mann ausgezogen ist, verhält die Ehefrau der Nachbarsfamilie sich mir gegenüber sehr distanziert."

Alleinerziehende fühlen sich häufig einsam und alleingelassen. Viele sind überfordert mit der alleinigen Verantwortung und dem Spagat zwischen Familien- und Erwerbsarbeit und der großen Belastung. Anstatt diese Arbeit anzuerkennen erleben Frauen häufig, dass sie defizitär gesehen werden.

Die oben stehenden Aussagen und meine Erfahrungen mit Alleinerziehenden in den vergangenen 16 Jahren werden untermauert durch rund 250 Gespräche mit Expert*innen, den Alleinerziehenden, sowie durch die intensive Kooperation von Netzanschluss mit dem Verband alleinerziehender Mütter und Väter, dem Jobcenter, der Agentur für Arbeit, dem Frauennetzwerk der Städteregion Aachen, der Diakonie, dem Caritasverband und weiteren Trägern, die Ansprechpartner für Alleinerziehende sind sowie Literatur, die am Ende des Artikels aufgeführt ist, insbesondere durch die aktuelle Studie „Alleinerziehend-Situation und Bedarfe (VAMV, 2019).

Die beschriebene Problematik der finanziellen und sozialen Armut Alleinerziehender haben die evangelischen und katholischen Kirchengemeinden im Aachener Westen auch wahrgenommen. Das veranlasste sie, ein Stadtteilnetzwerk für Alleinerziehende zu initiieren. Bevor ich dies vorstelle, möchte ich, zum besseren Verständnis, die Struktur des Stadtviertels beschreiben.

Beschreibung des Stadtviertels

Entwicklung des Stadtviertels Vaalserquartier

Das Stadtteilnetzwerk „Netzanschluss," das in diesem Artikel vorgestellt wird, liegt in Aachen, einer Stadt in Deutschland am Dreiländereck Deutschland, Niederlande, Belgien. Ganz im Westen der Stadt gibt es das Stadtviertel Vaalserquartier, in dem „Netzanschluss" beheimatet ist. Vaalserquartier ist ein Wohnviertel, das geprägt ist durch die kulturelle Vielfalt der Menschen, die hier leben. Um dies besser verstehen zu können, hier eine kurze Beschreibung zur Entwicklung des Stadtviertels, entnommen Pelzer (1985), ergänzt durch Aussagen von Zeitzeugen, insbesondere von Herrn André Krützen:

„Nach dem 2. Weltkrieg lebten etwa 2600 Menschen in Alt-Vaalserquartier, verteilt auf insgesamt 30 Bauernhöfe oder in kleinen zusammenhängenden Wohnsiedlungen. Das kleine Stadtviertel lag eingebettet zwischen Wiesen und Feldern an der niederländischen Grenze, etwa 8 km vom Aachener Zentrum entfernt. Es gab eine kleine Kirche, eine kleine Schule, eine geteerte Straße, ansonsten Feldwege. Gegenseitige nachbarschaftliche Unterstützung war selbstverständlich. In den 1960er Jahren hatten sich viele Höfe an ihre Existenzgrenze gewirtschaftet. Viele Bauernhöfe wurden aufgegeben, zu Wohnhäusern umgebaut und in den 1965er Jahren wurde mit der Besiedlung mehrerer kleinen Straßen begonnen. Aufgrund ihrer Insellage fernab von weiterer Zivilisation, identifizierten sich die Bewohner*innen sehr mit ihrem Stadtviertel. Mit dem Bau des Klinikums der RWTH (Rheinisch Westfälische Technische Hochschule) in den 1970 bis 1980er Jahren auf den Wiesen Vaalserquartiers jenseits der geteerten Straße, veränderte sich die Lebens- und Wohnsituation der Menschen in Alt-Vaalserquartier. Die Stadt Aachen gab die freien Flächen als Bauland frei. Ein alter Gutshof „Gut Kullen" wurde aufgegeben und gab dem neuen Wohngebiet seinen Namen. In kürzester Zeit begann die Besiedelung Gut Kullens mit dem Bau von Studenten- und Schwesternwohnheimen, vielen Nebengebäuden des medizinischen Versorgungsapparates, einigen Reihenhäusern und Doppel-haushälften, vielen Mehrfamilienhäusern, Wohnblocks und Sozial-wohnungen. Durch die Einrichtung eines Supermarktes, Geschäfte und Arztpraxen, Kindergärten, einer Jugendeinrichtung, einer Grundschule und einer evangelischen und einer katholischen Kirche wurde eine gute

Infra-struktur geschaffen. Studierende, Klinikum-Mitarbeiter*innen, kinderreiche Familien, Menschen mit Migrationshintergrund sowie viele Aussiedler-familien aus Polen und Russland haben hier ihre Heimat gefunden. Anfang der 1980er Jahre wurde weiteres Bauland freigegeben. Auf der Straßenseite von Alt-Vaalserquartier entstand der ‚Steppenberg' mit seinen Reihen-häusern, Doppelhaushälften und freistehenden Häusern. Mehrfamilienhäuser sind hier die Ausnahme. Für die Kinder der meist kinderreichen Familien wurden Kindertagesstätten errichtet. Außerdem ist auch hier ein Ärztehaus zu finden."

Wohn- und Lebenssituation im Stadtviertel

Die rasante Entwicklung des Stadtviertels Vaalserquartier durch die Entstehung von Gut Kullen und dem Steppenberg in den 1970/80er Jahren brachte bis zum heutigen Tag eine Vielzahl von Herausforderungen mit sich. Die geteerte große Straße existiert nach wie vor. Sie ist nicht nur eine Bundesstraße, die nach Vaals (NL) führt, sondern stellt für viele auch eine soziale Grenze dar. Interviews mit Trägern sozialer Einrichtungen, Geschäftsleuten und vor allem Stadtteilbewohner*innen (vgl. Overs & Patt-Wilhelm, 2001) bestätigen meinen persönlichen Eindruck.

Innerhalb der letzten 20 Jahre hat es einen demographischen Wandel im Stadtviertel gegeben. Die Bevölkerung des einst sehr kinderreichen Viertels ist immer älter geworden.

Während in Alt-Vaalserquartier nach wie vor viele „alteingesessene" Familien leben, deren Vorfahren früher Höfe besessen haben, wohnen am Steppenberg größtenteils zugezogene Akademiker*innen, viele mit Anstellung am Klinikum.

Gut Kullen hingegen zeichnet sich durch seine hohe Fluktuation und Multikulturalität aus. Hier leben, neben Studierenden aus aller Welt und einiger gut situierter Menschen, viele Familien, Geflüchtete und ältere Menschen, die Transferleistungen erhalten und an der Armutsgrenze leben. Um ein paar Zahlen zu nennen: In Gut Kullen leben 6697 Menschen, am Steppenberg und in Alt-Vaalserquartier 3299. 29,6% der Menschen aus Gut Kullen beziehen Transferleistungen, in den Bereichen Steppenberg und Alt-Vaalserquartier sind es 4,1 %. Als häufigste nicht-deutsche Nationalitäten sind in Gut Kullen China, Rumänien und Indien vertreten, am Steppenberg sind es die Niederlande, Frankreich, Rumänien und Belgien und in Alt-

Vaalserquartier Indien, China und die Niederlande. Während in Gut Kullen 26,2 % Alleinerziehende leben, sind es am Steppenberg und Alt-Vaalserquartier 19,4% (vgl. Sozialentwicklungsplan der Stadt Aachen, 2015).

Es wird deutlich, dass in Vaalserquartier auf wenigen Quadratkilometern Menschen unterschiedlicher sozialer und kultureller Herkunft und Lebensgeschichten zusammenleben, arme und reiche Menschen, mit ganz unterschiedlichen Möglichkeiten der gesellschaftlichen Teilhabe an Bildung und Kultur, Leben am Existenzminimum oder im Überfluss. Das Zusammenleben vieler sehr unterschiedlicher Menschen ist nicht immer leicht, teilweise wird es als bedrohlich und belastend erlebt. Meine persönliche Meinung dazu ist, dass es häufig eine Frage des Blickwinkels ist, wie wir Situationen einschätzen. Wir können Unterschiedlichkeiten als Trennendes, aber auch als Bereicherndes erleben und erkennen. In meiner Arbeit schätze ich die Diversität sehr, da sie eine Ressource darstellt. Auf diesen Aspekt gehe ich später genauer ein.

Die soziale Grenze der Vaalser Straße gibt es nach wie vor. Viel Engagement der Mitarbeiter*innen sozialer Einrichtungen und der Kirchengemeinden bietet den Bewohner*innen Möglichkeiten der Begegnung, des Austauschs und somit auch den Abbau von Vorurteilen. So werden soziale Brücken gebaut und Beziehungen geknüpft. Meiner Einschätzung nach leistet Netzanschluss hier einen großen Anteil.

Das Stadtteilnetzwerk „Netzanschluss"

Ausgangslage des Stadtteilnetzwerkes „Netzanschluss"

Seit Mitte der 1990er Jahre wurden die Kirchengemeinden im Aachener Westen durch Gespräche und „Hilferufe" zunehmend mit der besonderen Situation alleinerziehender Eltern konfrontiert. Sie sahen sich in der Verantwortung eine Antwort zu geben, sahen jedoch auch, dass ihre personellen Ressourcen eine entsprechende Unterstützung nicht ermöglichen konnten. So schlossen sich katholische und evangelische Kirchengemeinde zusammen, stellten eine Sozialpädagogin ein und gründeten im November 2004 „Netzanschluss" als ökumenisch getragene Anlaufstelle für

Alleinerziehende: Netz: etwas, das trägt und vernetzt – Anschluss: Kontakt, Anschluss bekommen.

Ende 2011 hat es in der Region Aachen eine repräsentative Befragung Alleinerziehender gegeben. Die Ergebnisse decken sich mit dem, was auch Mütter als Wünsche benennen, die zu uns kommen:

• Mehr Anerkennung der Alltagsleistung
• Mehr Möglichkeiten, qualifizierter Arbeit nachzugehen
• Mehr Teilhabemöglichkeiten am gesellschaftlichen Leben
• Bessere Möglichkeiten der Kinderbetreuung bzw. der Wunsch nach familienfreundlichen Arbeitszeiten.

Im Einvernehmen mit Kolleg*innen nehme ich zusätzlich wahr, wie einsam viele Mütter sind. Durch Trennung, Scheidung oder Tod des Partners sind viele häufig auf sich alleine gestellt, auf der dringenden Suche nach Kontakt; sie haben ein großes Bedürfnis nach Austausch und sind finanziell oft am Limit. „Es ist so schön, dass ich durch das Netzwerk andere Frauen in ähnlicher Situation kennen gelernt habe. Wir werden gemeinsam Silvester feiern – das erste Mal nach 8 Jahren, dass ich an dem Abend nicht alleine mit meinem Sohn bin." (Aussage einer 41jährigen Mutter des Netzwerkes).

Sorgen und Überforderung sind große Belastungen und machen häufig auch krank (VAMV, 2019). Begleitung und Unterstützung werden angefragt und angenommen.

Unsere Grundannahmen

Bei der Frage, wie brauchbare Unterstützung der Familien aussehen kann, beziehe ich mich gerne auf Louis Lowy, dessen Botschaft war:

> „Es ist die Hoffnung, die es Menschen ermöglicht, in Krisensituationen dennoch das eigene Leben in die Hand zu nehmen." (Ellerbrock, 2016)

Wie schaffen wir es, den Menschen ihre Zuversicht und Hoffnung nicht zu nehmen?

„Social groupwork," eine auf Emanzipation gerichtete und ressourcenorientierte Methode des sozialen Lernens, gibt mir hier eine Antwort (Nebel/Zinsheim, 1997). Zunächst ist es die Grundhaltung, nämlich mit den Klienten liebevoll, wertschätzend und humorvoll in Beziehung zu gehen. Jeder ist „richtig," so wie er ist, es wird nicht bewertet. Unsere Annahme ist, dass jeder Mensch alles mitbringt, was er braucht und die Lösung seines Problems in sich trägt. Meine Aufgabe sehe ich darin, die Klienten darin zu unterstützen, ihre Ressourcen wahrzunehmen und mit ihnen gemeinsam ein „Mehr an Möglichkeiten" zu schaffen. Zu einem respektvollen Umgang gehört auch, den Menschen nicht ihre Eigenverantwortlichkeit zu nehmen. Durch das Entdecken neuer Perspektiven sind sie meist wieder in der Lage, ihren persönlichen Weg zu erkennen, den sie ihrem Tempo entsprechend gehen dürfen. Dabei unterstütze ich dort, wo es nötig ist, lasse ihnen aber so viel Eigenverantwortung wie eben möglich. Meine Sicht auf die Dinge ist meine eigene Konstruktion. Ich kann nicht wissen, was für einen anderen brauchbar ist, aber ich kann Angebote machen. Der Klient selbst entscheidet was für ihn passt.

Beschreibung der Arbeit mit den damit verbundenen Zielen

Neben Einzelberatung, die bei mir im Büro stattfindet, gibt es kulturelle, informative und gesellige Angebote, mit und ohne Kinder – Möglichkeiten, sich zu informieren, kennen zu lernen, auszutauschen, anzufreunden, sich gegenseitig zu stärken und zu unterstützen. Die Treffen sind offen, jede(r) ist willkommen.

Da es sich bei den meisten Alleinerziehenden um Frauen handelt, werde ich der Einfachheit halber im folgenden Text von Frauen und Müttern sprechen, wohlwissend, dass sich auch gelegentlich Männer beteiligen.

Die Angebote und Treffen entwickeln sich aus den Bedarfen und werden mit den Familien gemeinsam entwickelt. Zu regelmäßig stattfindenden Treffen gehören zum Beispiel ein Frühstück und eine Frauengesprächsgruppe, die jeweils einmal im Monat angeboten werden, interkulturelles Kochen, Mutterverwöhnangebote wie Tagesausflüge, Kinobesuch, Wohlfühltage. Die Kinder werden dann bei Bedarf von Ehrenamtlichen betreut. Einmal jährlich fahren wir mit Frauen und Kindern für einen Tag an die holländische Nordsee. Wichtig ist mir, dass Teilnahme nie an finanziellen Gründen scheitert. Aufgrund großzügiger Spenden gut situierter Menschen des Stadtviertels, werden Unternehmungen stark bezuschusst, so dass nur noch ein für alle leistbarer Restbetrag von den Familien zu entrichten ist. Einen Eigenanteil beizusteuern hat für mich etwas mit einem würdevollen Umgang zu tun. Als Netzwerkskoordinatorin erhalte ich darüber hinaus immer wieder sehr brauchbare und gute Angebote. Neben reinen Spendengeldern erhalte ich auch Informationen von Vereinen, Firmen, Kulturstätten, die sich sozial engagieren und unterstützen. So gibt es beispielsweise vom Stadttheater Aachen eine Initiative, die stark reduzierte Eintrittskarten zur Verfügung stellt, Sportvereine, die einzelne Plätze für bedürftige Familien günstig anbieten oder soziale Clubs, die ein gezieltes Projekt unserer Initiative finanziell unterstützen.

Die Treffen in den Gruppen fördern sowohl die Identitätsbildung des Einzelnen als auch die aktive Auseinandersetzung zwischen den Mitgliedern einer Gruppe. Hier gibt es Raum, sich mit Betroffenen über Tabuthemen wie Armut auszutauschen, neue Kontakte zu knüpfen und Freundschaften aufzubauen.

Auch die Eltern stellen ihre Fähigkeiten dem Netzwerk zur Verfügung. Während die Teilnehmerinnen sich über die Angebote freuen, können die Verantwortlichen sich selbst in geschütztem Rahmen ausprobieren.

Dazu gehören beispielsweise:

* Handwerkerkurs (tapezieren, Umgang mit Bohrmaschinen)
* Goldschmiedeangebot
* Vortrag über Ernährung oder weitere Fachgebiete mit denen die Frauen vertraut sind
* Übernahme von Näharbeiten
* Kinderbetreuung
* Hilfe beim Umzug oder
* Haare schneiden.

Die Angebote finden zunächst im eigenen Netzwerk statt. Der weitere Schritt ist der, „nach außen" zu gehen und die Angebote für das Viertel zu öffnen. Frauen, die an Selbstbewusstsein verloren hatten, erleben sich häufig wieder neu und beginnen wieder, sich etwas zuzutrauen und an sich zu glauben.

Netzanschluss lebt vom Geben und Nehmen; die Familien erfahren praktische, organisatorische und emotionale Begleitung, umgekehrt profitieren die Kirchen und das Stadtviertel von dem ehrenamtlichen Engagement der Frauen z.B. „Partyservice" in der Gemeinde, Mitarbeit beim Basar, Unterstützung bei Gemeindefesten. Persönlich finde ich es wichtig, dass „die Alleinerziehenden ein Gesicht bekommen," dass gesehen und erfahren wird, was diese Frauen leisten, dass so manches Vorurteil zurechtgerückt wird.

Die Erfahrung zeigt, dass das Netzwerk mit den damit verbundenen Kontakten und Aktivitäten vielen zu dem Gefühl verhilft, nicht mehr alleine zu sein, dazu zu gehören, gesehen und gebraucht zu werden und neuen Lebensmut zu bekommen.

Café4You mit Kleiderlädchen

Ein wichtiges Projekt, das sich 2008 aus Netzanschluss entwickelt hat, ist das „Café4You" – ein soziales Café mit Kleiderlädchen. Bereits in den Jahren vor Gründung von Netzanschluss wurde in der Kirchengemeinde gebrauchte Kleidung für Bedürftige abgegeben, nach Entstehung von Netzanschluss vervielfachten sich diese Spenden. Außerdem bestand seit Langem der Bedarf nach einem Café im Viertel. „Hier im Viertel fehlt ein Café, das wir besuchen könnten, um mit anderen ins Gespräch zu kommen." (Aussage einer 62 jährigen Stadtteilbewohnerin, 2001). Und die Worte einer jungen Mutter (2004): „Es wäre schön einen offenen Treffpunkt zu haben, um andere Frauen aus dem Viertel kennen zu lernen." So wurde nach einer kurzen Vorbereitungszeit und kleinen räumlichen Veränderungen das Café4You in den Räumen der katholischen Kirchengemeinde im Bereich Gut Kullen eröffnet. Einmal wöchentlich ist es jeweils 2 Stunden am Vormittag und Nachmittag geöffnet. Weitere Informationen erhalten Interessierte über die Webseite der katholischen Kirchengemeinde (www.st.-konrad.de). Menschen verschiedener Kulturen und Generationen trinken hier zusammen Kaffee oder Tee. Es besteht die Möglichkeit des Austauschs und Kennenlernens, des „Sich informieren" und des Erzählens. Zur gleichen Zeit ist das gut sortierte, gepflegte und sehr ansprechende Kleiderlädchen geöffnet. Hier können Menschen zu einem kleinen Preis Kleidung einkaufen. Das Lädchen steht allen offen – egal wie hoch oder niedrig die finanziellen Möglichkeiten der Käufer sind. Die soziale Mischung der Kunden trägt zur Würde der finanziell benachteiligten Menschen bei. Hier muss sich keiner ausweisen, ob er berechtigt ist, einzukaufen. Außerdem haben wir, neben dem Aspekt günstig Kleidung zu erwerben, die Nachhaltigkeit im Blick. Pro Öffnungszeit sind 4 Ehrenamtliche im Einsatz, etwa ein Drittel von ihnen gehören Netzanschluss an.

Unsere Leitworte

Gemeinsam haben wir Leitworte formuliert, die die Bedeutung und Kultur von Netzanschluss deutlich machen sollen:

Ich Richtig Wichtig
Füreinander
Wir bewegen was
Spaß
Perspektivenwechsel
Hier geht was
Anschluss statt Kurzschluss

Zugehörigkeit und Vernetzung

Aktuell fühlen sich zugehörig:

- 44 alleinerziehende Frauen und zwei Männer mit ihren insgesamt 84 Kindern.
- Sie kommen aus verschiedenen sozialen Milieus, verfügen über Bildungsabschlüsse von Förderschule bis Hochschulstudium. 16 Frauen haben einen Migrationshintergrund (z.B. Türkei, Peru, Nordafrika, Kuba, Kamerun, Bosnien).
- Die jüngste Frau ist 22 Jahre alt, die älteste 58. Die meisten Frauen bleiben im Netzwerk, auch wenn ihre Kinder bereits von zuhause ausgezogen sind.
- Ehrenamtlich Tätige:
  Jugendliche und junge Erwachsene, die ansprechbar sind in Bezug auf Kinderbetreuung, Nachhilfe, Umzugshilfe, kleine handwerklichen Arbeiten, Transporte und ähnliches. Hier engagieren sich auch viele Kinder der Alleinerziehenden.
- 8 Frauen/Paare, die wie Großeltern die Familien unterstützen, mit ihnen feiern, für sie da sind, kostenfrei Nachhilfe erteilen, sie bei offiziellen Gesprächen unterstützen oder auch Behördengänge mit ihnen tätigen.
- Frauen und Männer, die bei handwerklichen Fragen und Problemen

tatkräftig unterstützen.

• Viele Menschen des Stadtviertels, die ihre Qualifikationen anbieten und bei Bedarf angefragt werden können (z.B. Juristen, Handwerker, PC-Fachleute, Ärzte, Bewerbungstrainerinnen).

• Menschen, die sich in unseren Emailverteiler haben aufnehmen lassen, über den Möbel, Jobs, Praktikumsstellen, Wohnungen und ähnliches angefragt werden können.

Als konkretes Beispiel der gegenseitigen Unterstützung innerhalb des Netzwerkes wird hier in Kurzform die Phase eines Umzugs einer alleinerziehenden Mutter beschrieben: Ehrenamtliche helfen beim Streichen und Böden verlegen. Über den Emailverteiler werden Möbel gesucht und gefunden und ein Umzugswagen organisiert. Am Umzugstag unterstützen Jugendliche und Männer, helfen beim Tragen und schleppen Kisten, die Frauen des Netzwerks bereits gepackt haben. Andere versorgen die Umzugshelfer mit Essen. Weitere Ehrenamtliche schließen Lampen an oder unterstützen Möbel aufzubauen. Die Koordination liegt bei der entsprechenden Frau. Sie hat die Helfer an ihrer Seite, aber sie ist für die Gesamtorganisation verantwortlich und bekommt so viel Unterstützung wie nötig und möglich.

Netzanschluss ist gut vernetzt mit den sozialen Einrichtungen und Beratungsstellen des Stadtviertels, ist Mitglied der Stadtteilkonferenz und des Frauennetzwerkes der Städteregion Aachen und hat sich sehr brauchbare Kooperationen mit anderen Trägern innerhalb der Stadt Aachen aufgebaut.

Netzanschluss ist im November letzten Jahres 15 Jahre alt geworden. Unter Mitwirkung aller Beteiligten arbeiten wir prozessorientiert und bedarfsorientiert. Von daher hat sich in den Jahren vieles verändert und konnte sich neu entwickeln. Anforderungen und Bedingungen verändern sich ständig. Ich bin sehr zuversichtlich, dass wir diesen auch weiterhin gemeinsam gewachsen sind.

Literaturverzeichnis

Bertelsmann Stiftung (Hrsg.) (2013). *LebensUmwege: Alleinerziehende: Zehn Porträts*. Gütersloh: Bertelsmann.
Butterwegge, C. (2001). „Teufelskreis Armut.“ Gewerkschaft Erziehung und

Wissenschaft, 5/2001.

Ministerium für Gesundheit, Soziales, Frauen und Familie des Landes NRW. (2004). *Frauenportraits – Lebensgeschichten alleinerziehender Migrantinnen und deutschen Frauen.*

Nebel, G. & Woltmann-Zingsheim, B. (Eds.) 1997). *Werkbuch für das Arbeiten mit Gruppen.* Aachen: Institut für Beratung und Supervision.

Overs, U. & Patt-Wilhelm, K. (2001). „Agatha, Wilhelmine, Konstantine Gräfin von und zu Vaalserquartier" – Konzeption und Durchführung eines Stadtteilprojektes zur Überwindung sozialer Grenzen innerhalb eines Wohngebietes." Diplomarbeit im Fachbereich Sozialwesen an der Katholischen Fachhochschule Aachen.

VAMV. (2016). *Alleinerziehend – Tipps und Informationen.* Verband Alleinerziehender Mütter und Väter, Bundesverband e.V. Ausgabe 22.

Internetquellenverzeichnis

Alleinerziehend – Situation und Bedarfe, 2019. Aktuelle Studienergebnisse zu Nordrhein-Westfalen und der Bundesrepublik Deutschland Erstellt im Auftrag von Verband alleinerziehender Mütter und Väter Landesverband Nordrhein-Westfalen e. V. Abgerufen von https://vamv-nrw.de/studie

Bertelsmannstudie / Lenze, Anne; Funke, Antje: Alleinerziehende unter Druck, Berlin. (2016). Abgerufen von https://www.bertelsmann-stiftung. de/de/publikationen/publikation/did/alleinerziehende-unter-druck-/1/

Café4You. Abgerufen von http://st-konrad-ac.de/gemeinde/einrichtungen/ cafe4you.php5

Demografischer Wandel Kompendium (Teil Familie) StädteRegion. (2014). Abgerufen von https://www.staedteregion-aachen.de/fileadmin/ user_upload/A

Fachausschuss „Alleinerziehende" des Frauennetzwerkes der Städteregion Aachen Abgerufen von www.forum-e.de

Familienbericht NRW. (2017). Abgerufen von https://www.mkffi.nrw/sites/ default/files/asset/document/familienbericht_kurzfassung_rz_neu. pdf und https://www.mkffi.nrw/sites/default/files/asset/document/ familienbericht_langfassung.pdf

Familienreport. (2017). Abgerufen von https://www.bmfsfj.de/blob/119524/ f51728a14e3c91c3d8ea657bb01bbab0/familienreport-2017-data.pdf

Jobcenter StädteRegion Aachen: Arbeitsmarkt- und Integrationsprogramm. (2018). Abgerufen von https://www.jobcenter-staedteregion- aachen.de/fileadmin/jobcenter/content/Arbeitsmarkt-_und_ Integrationsprogramm_2018.pdf

Kindesunterhalt: Warum viele Väter nicht zahlen. (2016). Abgerufen von https://www.t-online.de/leben/familie/erziehung/id_76854700/

kindesunterhalt-warum-viele-vaeter-nicht-zahlen-wollen.html

Informationen des Bundesamtes für Arbeit und Soziales. Abgerufen von www.bmas.de

Informationen zum Thema foodsharing. Abgerufen von https://foodsharing. de

Informationen zum Thema Kinderbetreuung. Abgerufen von https://www. vamv.de/allein-erziehen/kinderbetreuung/

Informationen zum Thema „Tafeln." Abgerufen von http://www.production. tafel.de/themen/armut/kinderarmut/

Medien zum Thema Armut – Nachrichtenarm. Mit Maja Malik über Armut in den Medien. Abgerufen von https://dasneue.berlin/2019/06/11/ dnb032-nachrichtenarm/

Mehrkindfamilien in Deutschland. (2013). Abgerufen von https:// www.bmfsfj.de/blob/94312/0b8bf636b124a2735ed0f46ed4e80bfe/ mehrkindfamilien-in-deutschland-data.pdf

Sozialentwicklungsplan. (2015). Abgerufen von www.aachen.de/DE/ stadt_buerger/.../sozialentwicklungsplan_neu/index.html

Studie Entwicklung der Einkommenssituation von Familien. (2018). https:// www.bertelsmannstiftung.de/fileadmin/files/Projekte/Familie_und_ Bildung/Studie_WB_Einkommenssituation_von_Familien_2018.pdf

Thesen zur Flüchtlingsarbeit in Deutschland. (2016). Abgerufen von https:// www.iaswg.de/thesen-zur-fluechtlingsarbeit-in-deutschland/

Verband alleinerziehender Mütter und Väter. Abgerufen von www.vamv.de

Group work course design bridged: Experiences from Canada and South Africa

Roshini Pillay and Sarah LaRocque

Introduction

Groups are a cornerstone of social work practice, providing diversity in function and formats at the macro, mezzo, and micro levels. Zastrow (2012) defines these three levels of social work intervention as being micro work on a one-to-one basis with an individual, mezzo as working with families and other small groups, and macro as working towards social change in the community, and with organizations. In an increasingly global community, we need to understand and respect the influence of diversity and social justice in group dynamics as groups are often a microcosm of the social environment in which they take place. As social group workers and educators, we need to continually identify and respond to issues of social justice that "represent social inequities of power, privilege, and oppression" (Miller et al., 2004, p. 377). Recognizing one's social location and how this impacts a group's dynamics is part of group work.

A strength-based approach that supports the empowerment of all group members requires students to first understand their own lived experiences with power and privilege and how this impacts what they bring to groups as facilitators. Training students in course and field education is a complex process that involves an interplay between the acquisition and application of empirical knowledge and technical skills, alongside personal growth, and development of professional uses of self. This article presents the experiences of two social work educators in Canada and South Africa and the course design and training choices they make to ensure that students become co-creators of knowledge and learning by doing and learning from working in a group.

Who we are?

We are group work practitioners grounded in the real-world and have spent a considerable amount of time practicing as social workers before becoming social work academics. This exposure has honed our mutual passion for learning and teaching methods based on experiential learning within the contextual reality of the world of work. In writing together, we see our work as giving meaning to the theme of this conference which was bridging the divide through the collaborative sharing of group work curriculum design.

Sarah was also keen to develop the bridge between South Africa and Canada and this resulted in us co-presenting a workshop at the IASWG conference held in 2018 in the Kruger National Park. This was how this paper emerged whereby our mutual interest in group work education grew. While vast geographical spaces and time zones separate us, the aspect that binds us is the desire to develop new ways to teach group work in a changing world where diversity is under threat from nationalist movements.

At a pragmatic level, there is a desire to ensure that theories, activities and course design strategies have real-world relevance so that students can engage with the material as they learn in a manner that is experiential and evidence-based. We as educators know that students are never passive recipients of knowledge and strive to ensure that the activities and tasks we design get students to work on solving and learning skills that are necessary for practice and reflect their lived experiences with groups.

For this article, the Canadian focus is field education and the South African focus is teaching group work theory; we recognize, however, that these aspects are integrated and inseparable because social work is a practicing profession (Teater, 2011). Moreover, the challenge in social work education has often been finding ways so that students can better integrate theory with practice. Thus, in this paper, we discuss the linkages between our teaching practices from Canada to South Africa.

In our teaching practices, we adopt a situated cognitive learning style that considers the contextual factors that interact with knowledge development while subscribing to a cognitive apprenticeship approach (Brown, Collins, & Duguid, 1989; Mattar, 2018). Cognitive apprenticeship is the process of embedding "learning in activity and making deliberate use of the social and physical context" (ibid., 1989, p. 32). The course design process may include reflection, learning with technology, access to expert performance, scaffolding and coaching, iteration, multiple perspectives, working on a real-world problem over a sustained period, and seamless assessment as some of the elements of authentic learning (Herrington, Reeves & Oliver, 2010). The cognitive apprenticeship approach and elements of authentic learning consider social interactions as well as shared knowledge through group work exercises. A critical aspect of these learning designs is the types of interactions that are developed in a group. Zastrow (2012) confirms that social work students benefit from "experiential training in classes to prepare them for the realities of social work practice" (p. 24).

The workplace realities need to be brought into the class through real-world examples and situations. In group work, there is an added benefit of getting students to work collaboratively in that they hone their skills, develop cohesion, have fun, and learn from each other before they go into the real world. It is important to note that through the power of praxis, students may facilitate group work at their field placement and can make connections between the real world and the classroom. In so doing classroom and theoretical knowledge are deepened and enriched.

When considering how the classroom becomes an experiential learning space, consideration is given to the following aspects:

- Understanding the learning needs of students,
- Carefully designing course activities and exercises that have pedagogical value and articulating this value to the students,
- Acknowledging that some exercises may be uncomfortable and allowing students the space to discuss this on a one-on-one basis,
- The creation of the classroom as a safe, caring, respectful and supportive space for development and learning,
- Conveying to the students the value and limits of confidentiality in the classroom space,
- Being authentic to encourage critical self-reflection as group members,
- Offering guidance in a developmental way by the educators and the peers,
- Seeing the value of critical self-reflection in group process,
- Supporting personal growth to foster professional development.

These are the aspects that bridge the divide in our course designs for group work education in the classroom and field education.

Group work education experience in Canada

As a field educator I am a strong proponent of group training, understanding the effectiveness of groups in mental health and social services (Burlingame, Fuhriman, & Mosier, 2003). Being tasked with the responsibility of providing comprehensive teaching in social group work in real-world practice is complex. Training often entails starting at the foundational level in group theory, process, and research-informed practice, while providing continuous opportunities for students to engage in experiential learning to bridge classroom learnings with direct practice. Field practicums can accomplish this educational aspect of social group work by providing (a) direct group experience as opposed to observation only, (b) opportunities for personal growth and professional development, and (c) knowledge translation strategies.

Direct group experience

Group trainers such as Markus and Abernethy (2001), St. Pierre (2014), and Tschuschke and Greene (2002) recommend opportunities for students to participate as group members to foster the group membership experience, engage in critical self-reflection, personal growth, and development of professional uses of self. Cohen (2004), Ieva et al. (2009), and Yalom and Leszcz (2005) argue that emotional experiencing is optimally discovered in a naturalistic way during group training, rather than in simulations or through observation alone. In my experience students are often anxious about their ability to appropriately self-disclose, practice competently, and regulate negative affective states that may be triggered in groups. Research suggests that direct group experience without the responsibility of facilitation provides students with cognitive apprenticeship and an experiential understanding of the change process in groups (LaRocque, 2018; Weiss & Rutan, 2016).

Personal and professional growth

When group trainees learn to identify, understand, and debrief their patterned feeling states, affect, and ways of relating to others through the lens of critical reflection, they build professional uses of self (Vito, 2015; Zhu, 2018). It is well documented that the group facilitator-member relationship is related to both member and group outcomes, regardless of theoretical orientation, group function, or format. Therefore, learning self-containment and differential uses of self is considered an essential component for students in field education (Beck & Lewis, 2000; Flores, 2017; Markin & Marmarosh, 2012; Shectman & Toren, 2009). Group educators and researchers such as Brabender (2010), Kivligan and Tibbits (2012), Markin and Marmarosh (2010), Pelech et al. (2016), and St. Pierre (2014) recommend that students engage in personal growth to identify, understand, accept, and contain their emotional reactions in groups. Despite the support in the literature for group participation as a key instructional method in supporting personal growth and development of professional uses of self in group education, there has been surprisingly limited research dedicated to this component of group training, and little consensus on how to integrate personal and professional development in group training in field education (Ieva et al., 2009; Kivligan & Tibbits, 2012; Lau et al., 2010). Zhu's (2018) review of experiential growth groups in counselor education noted that there does "not appear to be pedagogical guidelines" on the format, facilitation, or purpose of experiential groups (p. 145).

Most of the literature on experiential training in professional uses of self in groups is descriptive, anecdotal, and based on authoritative consensus (Macgowan, 2012; Pelech et al., 2016; Zhu, 2018). Although there is limited research on how uses of self, clinical judgment, and group facilitator individuality impact outcomes in groups, there is renewed emphasis on experiential learning in group training that attends to personal growth and professional uses of self (Heydt & Sherman, 2005; Ieva et al., 2009; Knight, 2014; Lau, Ogrodniczuk, Joyce, & Sochting, 2010; McCarthy, Falco, & Villaba, 2014). Expert consensus does suggest, however, that developing self-awareness is essential for students to understand:

• the change process in groups;
• the risks involved in self-disclosure and trust;

- the impact of respectful beliefs, values, and a non-judgmental stance on the working alliance;
- the importance of empathizing with members' struggles; and
- the need to contain emotions and delay behaviors so as not to impose the group facilitator's needs on the group-as-a-whole (Bernard et al., 2008; Kivligan & Tibbits, 2012; Ieva et al., 2009; Pelech et al., 2016; Stone & Spielberg, 2009; Yalom & Leszcz, 2005).

Knowledge translation

Knowledge translation is an essential step in developing structural knowledge, and group trainees who use research to inform practice are more likely to engage in evidence-based practice (Kivlighan & Tibbits, 2012). Traditionally, field educators relied on course instruction to prepare students for real-world practice in groups. In Canada and the United States, there is a decline in group courses in social work concurrent to an increasing reliance on field instructors to provide group education and training (Ayala et al., 2018; Knight, 2014; McNicoll & Lindsay, 2002; Sweifach, 2014) in the context of reported decreasing practicum instructors and sites (Knight, 2014; Hadjipavlou, Kealy, & Ogrodniczuk, 2017; Vito, 2015). It is within this contextual reality that I began to explore participant observation as a method of training in field education to support students' cognitive apprenticeship of social group work. I will focus here on a method of training in field education that I have adapted specifically to support personal growth and the development of uses of self as a social group worker while using a knowledge translation tool that supports cognitive apprenticeship.

Participant observation in group training

I began to explore participant observation as a method of training in groups several years ago and have been refining the teaching/learning techniques ever since. The concept of participant observation comes from qualitative research literature, specifically ethnographic research (Wilson, 2008). It is designed to provide rich information on a complex phenomenon, mainly the social behaviors and mental actions (such as ideas and beliefs) of an identifiable group of persons in a naturalistic setting (Creswell, 2013; van Manen, 1990). Wilson (2008), in describing indigenous research methods, described participant observation as "watching and doing" by engaging with the study group in their activities while "simultaneously observing their behavior and analyzing why they are doing things in their way" (p. 40). In my experience as a group trainer, students naturally flow between participant observation activities when allowed to directly experience a group without facilitation responsibilities. With each group session, they learn to use their internal responses to understand the power of group dynamics on members, reflect on personal biases, beliefs, and values, and the change process. It is important to orient students to identify and understand important moments in a group's interactions that trigger intense emotional reactions for them. This is their intrapersonal and interpersonal learning as a group member. Students learn to use participant observation to orient to relational group themes and dynamics, observe professional group facilitators' use of techniques in complex interactions, and link theory with intervention. By immersing group trainees as participant observers in groups in real-world practice, they can experientially participate in the process and interactions, gaining first-hand knowledge of group membership, the change process, and the impact of the group facilitators' interventions.

As observers, the students filter the group's interactions, and their own experiences, through group theories and models. Weiss and Rutan (2016) found similar results in their study. McGovern (2016), in her series of seven books on social work placement, suggests that observation of skilled professionals should be an important component of training. This process supports group trainees linking research and theories with their group experiences in real-time. I have found that students individualize this aspect of their training, reflecting cognitive apprenticeship. Students are more motivated to seek out research, authoritative texts, and relevant podcasts when they are guiding their own learning goals. To support the knowledge translation process in the context of field education, I adapted Bogo and Vayda's (1989) Integration of Theory and Practice Model to group work. As can be ascertained, the table's format supports research-informed practice, as opposed to the more difficult format to implement evidence-based practice.

By combining participant observation with research-informed learning I feel I am providing foundational instruction in real-world practice. An essential aspect of professional development in group training is teaching social work students how to develop professional uses of self as an instrument of change in groups (Shechtman & Toren, 2009). The process involves students' purposeful observations of their thoughts, emotions, assumptions, biases, and actions in response to group dynamics. In groups, facilitators need to be aware of emotional phenomena, biases, privileges, and systemic injustices that may distort their ability to remain helpful to the group (Caplan & Thomas, 2002; Flores, 2017; Furman et al., 2014; Tibbits, 2012; Lau et al., 2010; Pelech et al., 2016; St. Pierre, 2014).

Among the few studies that have investigated personal growth and professional uses of self in group training, researchers have found positive outcomes on group dynamics and student learning (Doel, 2006; Ieva et al., 2009; Stempler, 1993; Zhu, 2018). Any concerns that I initially entertained around students engaging in personal therapy or pressure on dual relationship boundaries were quickly allayed. As Cohen (2004) wrote, students understand the difference between personal therapy and personal growth leading to professional development and respect the authentic learning environment. As a field educator in the age of neoliberalism and competing for inclusive practice, participant observation humanizes teaching and learning and opens dialogues in groups that reflect the communities that social work students practice in.

Group work education experience in South Africa

As a social work educator who teaches group work theory to undergraduate students in South Africa, I am acutely aware of the role played by social justice and participatory parity (Fraser, 1996) in supporting students to achieve academic success. South Africa is still in the throes of transformation since the apartheid era. The contextual reality is that many of the students I encounter are from resource-scarce backgrounds and are the first in their families to enter university. Therefore, the lived experiences of the students need to be part of the learning and teaching process. I am of the view that sound pedagogy needs to support decisions for course design.

I believe that course design strategies need to incorporate

meaningful activities, thus teaching group work is enhanced when students engage in similar activities while they learn. Therefore, course design should replicate some of the activities conducted in the real world, so that students can rehearse and develop skills mastery in their chosen profession (Herrington, Reeves & Oliver, 2010). Critical to course development are the methods used for learning and teaching, including the use of participatory learning and action techniques that provide students with experiential learning.

Authentic learning elements for group work

Group work education based on the undergraduate curriculum in the social work department where I teach begins in the second year of the four-year degree and ends in the fourth year. The educator responsible for field instruction and I reviewed the course design process. Next, I outline these course design principles based on the Authentic Learning Framework (Herrington, Reeves & Oliver, 2010) that I found to be useful for student engagement in group work education.

Authentic activities provide the opportunity to collaborate

Students should be divided into groups to develop group work skills. Courses should be designed so that opportunities are created for students to collaborate and share ideas and information (Herrington, 2006; Lave & Wenger, 1991). Activities should be designed to facilitate the development of rapport and group cohesion, both in face-to-face and online spaces (Corey, Corey, & Corey, 2010; Rouke & Anderson, 2003).

Real-world relevance

The groups of students should choose a social condition about which they are interested and motivated to learn more, from within the South African context. In this way the social condition is part of the South African context, enabling students to feel an emotional attachment or connection to their complex task (Rule, 2006; Wetherell, 2012).

Authentic activities provide the opportunity to develop skills in social work

Students need to develop social work skills, ethics, and values that prepare them for practice. Courses should be designed to foster discipline-specific professional values and make use of real-world examples. Experiential learning and role-play should be used to allow students to engage and perform in class. Students learn about group work while working in a group and in their process of being inducted into the profession of social work (Wenger, 2006).

Authentic activities provide the opportunity to reflect

Diversity in the learning environment should be appreciated, and opportunities for developing reflection in students should be included. Students should be engaged in activities that facilitate critical reflection and link this type of reflection to the discipline-specific values of being a reflective practitioner in social work. Students ought to be encouraged to pay attention to both reflections in and on the process (Schön, 2011). When using deep reflection, the role played by emotion should be acknowledged. Safe spaces in the learning environment should be created.

Authentic activities provide opportunities for creative problem-solving

Course design should consider the needs of individual students despite class sizes being large. The course must allow for problem-solving creativity and flexibility and allow students to make their paths to finding solutions (Herrington, Reeves & Oliver, 2010).

Authentic activities are conducive to communication and learning

The educator must encourage debate, articulation and role modeling by the educator and the students (Herrington, Reeves & Oliver, 2010; Wenger, 2006; Zeman & Swanke, 2008). The educator should allow for conflict and encourage students to not take criticism personally.

Authentic activities should be examined from different perspectives

Students should have access to multiple platforms and resources that include Technology Enhanced Learning (TEL). These multiple perspectives allow for competing solutions and diversity of outcomes, thus encouraging flexibility and acknowledgment of the views of group members (Brown, Collins, & Duguid, 1989; Herrington, Reeves, & Oliver, 2006).

An authentic task is ill-defined and complex

A group work course should include multiple activities, role-play and experiential learning and students should have the opportunity to choose their learning path and their own topic and take ownership of their learning and the learning of their members (Herrington, Reeves & Oliver, 2010).

Course design should be informed by sound pedagogical theory (Herrington, Reeves & Oliver, 2010). The educator must have passion and knowledge of the subject and infuse this knowledge of the subject in teaching while making explicit to students the reasons for course design strategies. The use of these design elements supports the experiential learning process that we as educators value.

Conclusion

This paper shows the value of experiential learning for group work education in theory and field instruction and offers the reader a novel perspective of engaging students while learning by doing. Our common goal as social work educators is to develop reflective and reflexive student social workers who value social justice and emerge as effective social workers in the real world. It is envisaged that the methods we have highlighted can be adapted by other educators in different settings.

References

Ayala, J., Drolet, J., Fulton. A., Hewson, J., Letkemann, L., Baynton, M., Elliott, G., Judge-Stasiak, A., Blaug, C., Gérard Tétreauit, A., & Schweizer, E. (2018). Restructuring social work field education in 21st Century Canada: From crisis management to sustainability. *Canadian Social Work Review, 35*(2), 45–65. https://doi.org/10.7202/1058479ar

Bogo, M. (2006). Field instruction in social work. *The Clinical Supervisor, 24*(1–2), 163–193.

Brooks, J., McCluskey, S., Turley, E., & King, N. (2015). The utility of template analysis in qualitative psychology research. *Qualitative Research in Psychology, 12*, 202–222.

Brown, J. S., Collins, A., & Duguid, P. (1989). Situated cognition and the culture of learning. *Educational Researcher, 18*(1), 32–42.

Burlingame, G. M., Fuhriman, A., & Mosier, J. (2003). The differential effectiveness of group psychotherapy: A meta-analytic perspective. *Group Dynamics: Theory, Research, and Practice, 7*(1), 3–12.

Doel, M. (2006). *Using group work*. New York, NY: Routledge.

Flores, P. J. (2017). Attachment theory and group psychotherapy. *International Journal of Group Psychotherapy, 67*, S50–S59.

Fraser, N. (1996). Social Justice in the Age of Identity Politics: Redistribution Recognition, and Participation. Paper presented at the Tanner Lectures on Human Values.

Furman, R., Bender, K., & Rowan, D. (2014). *An experiential approach to group work* (2nd ed.). New York, NY: Oxford University Press.

Herrington, J. (2006). *Authentic e-learning in higher education: Design principles for authentic learning environments and tasks*. Paper presented at the World Conference on E-Learning in Corporate, Government, Healthcare, and Higher Education (ELEARN), Honolulu, Hawaii, USA.

Herrington, J., Reeves, T., & Oliver, R. (2006). Authentic tasks online: A synergy among learner, task, and technology. *Distance Education, 27*(2), 233–247.

Herrington, J., Reeves, T., & Oliver, R. (2010). *A guide to authentic e-learning*. New York, NY: Routledge.

Heydt, M. J. & Sherman, N. E. (2005). Conscious use of self: Tuning the instrument of social work practice with cultural competence. *The Journal of Baccalaureate Social Work, 10*(2), 25–40.

Knight, C. (2014). Teaching group work in the BSW generalist social work curriculum: Core content. *Social Work with Groups, 37*(1), 25–35.

LaRocque, S. (2018). A thematic analysis of group trainees and trainers' experiences of the participant observer group training framework (Doctoral thesis). ProQuest Dissertations and Theses database.

Lau, M. A., Ogrodniczuk, J., Joyce, A. S., & Sochting, I. (2010). Bridging the practitioner-scientists gap in group psychotherapy research. *International Journal of Group Psychotherapy, 60*(2), 177–196.

Lave, J. & Wenger, E. (1991). *Situated Learning. Legitimate peripheral participation.* Cambridge, England: University of Cambridge.

McGovern, M. (2016). *Social work placement: New approaches. New thinking. 2. Assessment, creative supervision, feedback.* Retrieved from https://www.amazon.ca/Social-Work-Placement- Approaches-Thinking ebook/dp/B077NJHV78/ref=sr_ 1_ 1?s= books & ie = UTF8&qid=1518305200&sr=1-1 & keywords= social+work + placement % 3A + New +Approaches

Mattar, J. (2018). Constructivism and connectivism in education technology: Active, situated, authentic, experiential, and anchored learning. *RIED. Revista Iberoamericana de Educación a Distancia, 21*(2), 201–217.

Miller, J., Donner, S., & Fraser, E. (2004) Talking when talking is tough: Taking on conversations about race, sexual orientation, gender, class and other aspects of social identity, *Smith College Studies in Social Work, 74*(2), 377–392. DOI: 10.1080/00377310409517722

Pelech, W., Basso, R., Lee, C. D, & Gandarilla, M. (2016). *Inclusive group work.* New York, NY: Oxford University Press.

Rouke, L. & Anderson, T. (2003). Using Peer Teams to Lead Online Discussions. *Journal of Interactive Media in Education, 1*, 1–21.

Rule, A. C. (2006). The components of authentic learning. *Journal of Authentic Learning, 3*(1), 1–10.

Schön, D. (2011). *The reflective practitioner: how professionals think in action* (Reprinted ed.). Farnham: Ashgate.

Shechtman, Z. & Toren, Z. (2009). The effect of leader behavior on processes and outcomes in group counselling. *Group Dynamics, Theory, Research, and Practice, 13*(3), 218–233.

Stempler, B. J. (1993). Supervisory co-leadership. *Social Work with Groups, 16*(3), 97–110.

Sweifach, J. (2014). Group work education today: A content analysis of MSW group work course syllabi. *Social Work with Groups, 37*(1), 8–22

Teater, B. (2011). Maximizing student learning: A case example of applying teaching and learning theory in social work education. *Social Work Education, 1*, 1–15.

Tschuschke, V. & Greene, L. R. (2002). Group therapists' training: What predicts learning? *International Journal of Group Psychotherapy, 52*(4), 463–482.

Vito, R. (2015). Leadership support of supervision in social work practice: Challenges and enablers to achieving success. *Canadian Social Work Review, 32*(2), 151–165.

Wenger, E. (Producer). (2006). Communities of Practice: A Brief Introduction. [Self-published report]. Retrieved from www.ewenger.com

Weiss, A. C. & Rutan, J. S. (2016). The benefits of group therapy observation for therapists-in-training. *International Journal of Group Psychotherapy, 66*(2), 246–260.

Wetherell, M. (2012). *Affect and emotion: A new social science understanding*: Sage Publications.

Zastrow, C. (2012). Social work with groups: a comprehensive worktext (8th ed.). Belmont, CA: Brooks/Cole, Cengage Learning.

Zeman, L. & Swanke, J. (2008). Integrating Social Work Practice and Technology Competencies: A Case Example. *Social Work Education, 27*(6), 601–612.

Group work education: Teaching through team-based learning to promote social justice in the learning community

Marie Ubbink and Gerda Reitsma

Introduction

Nelson Mandela said: "Education is the most powerful weapon that you can use to change the world." However, educational systems are failing many young people who face a range of social and economic challenges in their communities daily due to multiple forms of injustice (Mills & McGregor, 2013). This is especially true for South Africa. Many of the students attending higher education institutes come from disadvantaged milieus (Cross & Carpentier, 2009). Ross (2010) identified some of these injustices that social work students were experiencing in their home communities, such as poverty, absence of a parent(s), caring for siblings, lack of basic facilities at home and school, language difficulties and the trauma of rape. Cross and Carpentier (2009) explain that these students are less prepared for the challenges of university studies. Sennet, Finchilescu, Gibson and Strauss (2003) found in their study on African students' experiences at a South African University that the students experienced some personal-emotional anxiety and social adjustment problems. They also reported a significant relationship between students' experiences of violence and disruptions in their home communities and poor academic performances.

Sennet et al. (2003) state that universities need to give equal consideration to the environmental determinants of students' adjustment as to those arising from the individual's background and life circumstances. Universities have been implementing various processes and procedures to provide access to more students (Cele & Menon, 2006), however, the challenge is to provide effective support to these students to also be successful in their studies. Institutional support in the form of additional programmes, student support services, and financial support may be available, but another level of support is needed in the classroom (the environment) where the students are expected to study and function daily.

Sennet et al. (2003) report that many students from previously disadvantaged communities feel alienated from their lecturers, which can impact their learning negatively. Implementing a pedagogy that promotes collaboration and active learning may create an environment where students feel engaged and part of the learning process, especially where some form of peer teaching takes place (Snyder, Sloane, Dunk & Wiles, 2016). Collaborative learning is the grouping and pairing of students to achieve a learning goal. The advantages of engaging students in collaborative learning during teaching and learning has been motivated through various studies (Laal & Ghodsi, 2012; Terenzini, Cavrera, Colbeck, Parente, & Bjorklund, 2001). The principle of collaborative learning is based on organised student groups working on structured tasks where they must work together to reach a goal, solve a problem, make a decision or create a product. The learners are responsible for one another's learning as well as their own (Laal & Ghosdi, 2012). Jacobs, Vakalisa and Gawe (2011, p. 197) explain that "students are responsible for learning and for helping their fellow group members to learn or practice skills. There is a strong emphasis on cooperation and interdependence of group members." Collaborative learning provides a learning situation where students work together cooperatively to accomplish shared learning goals (Scager, Boonstra, Peeters & Wiegant, 2016), implying that a form of active learning is taking place (Johnson & Johnson, 2009).

Snyder et al. (2016) explain that collaborative peer learning creates an environment conducive to social networking and reinforcement of disciplinary field identity. According to Wiese et al. (2015), students develop social networks during collaborative learning, for example in Team-Based Learning (TBL). A social network creates a peer support system that can help students adapt to the learning environment (Wiese et al., 2015). TBL promotes the development of critical thinking and teamwork skills and emotional intelligence in health professions students (Sands & Solomon, 2003; Wilson-Delfosse 2012). With TBL, student engagement and satisfaction in the learning process increase. TBL re-engages young people who have become disenchanted with traditional teaching into the learning process (Mills & McGregor, 2013) and improves their learning (Eksteen, Reitsma, Swart & Fourie, 2018).

Traditional lecture methods are teacher-centred and discipline-based. TBL aims to ensure students engage deeper with course content through collaborative learning. Research on TBL had shown that this approach is an effective teaching strategy for involving students in their learning process. This article provides a brief insight into the educational practice of TBL that can function as a pedagogy to help students create social support networks as a form of classroom-level support. The TBL methodology provides a coherent framework for building an entire course experience, which may differ from other forms of collaborative learning (Sibley et al., 2014). In this article, we explore how TBL can be applied in a second-year social work course to promote collaboration, improve learning, and develop social networks for student support.

Context of the Social Work Module

One of the modules in the Bachelor of Social Work (BSW) programme is a Social Work Therapeutic / Treatment Group work module presented in the second year of the undergraduate programme. Group therapy is considered one of the promising psychosocial treatment modalities which are practiced in clinical settings for persons with emotional problems or mental health issues by qualified mental health professionals such as psychiatrists, clinical psychologists, psychiatric nurses, psychiatric social workers and occupational therapists specialised in mental health. The group therapist is an active participant in the group and helps its members to understand their problems as well as interpersonal problems. Group discussions are focused on current problems concerning oneself and others. Group therapy aims to bring about a reduction in symptoms such as negative symptoms, poor motivation, as well as improvement in social functioning, better adjustment, and improved interpersonal relationship skills (Ezhumalai, Muralidhar, Dhanasekarapandian & Nikketha, 2018). In social work, this form of group therapy is implemented as treatment groups. Treatment groups, as a primary method applied in social work, is practiced with persons with minor adjustment problems to function well. The social worker as facilitator acts as an enabler; enabling the group members to plan, organise and execute the group programme activities that will help them with their personal growth and development (Ezhumalai et al., 2018).

For social work students to understand and implement therapeutic treatment groups in practice successfully, they should have experienced successful group work techniques during their undergraduate training. However, it became clear that the current pedagogy applied in the 2nd year Social Work Therapeutic Group Work course was not successful in providing students with positive experiences of group work. Group work activities were limited (more time was spent on lectures) and not successful as students showed resistance to working in groups. Penn (2017) mentions that group work should have the following elements: members should be contributing to the group's work; the interaction between group members; how the group focuses; should expect quality; high expectations of what the group can produce; must possess relevant knowledge, skills and competencies; conflict management; respect for others; and a focus on problem-solving. Currently, the group work in the second-year module does not meet these requirements. Students are dissatisfied with group assignments as most of the criteria listed by Penn (2017) were not met. The theory is not mastered by all group members, especially during the written assignments. Not all students have acquired the knowledge or skills and the abilities that are expected, and therefore the theory was not understood. The group assignment problems caused conflict and communication problems between the students, and the group presentations were not prepared with care as a result of the conflict, as was visible with the presentation and the assessment marks allocated.

The students did not enjoy the group work in class, there was a lack of student engagement, mostly surface learning took place and the lecturer had to constantly try and motivate them to work in their groups. The impact this negative attitude had on their learning about an essential Social Work Therapeutic Group Work method (module content) was a concern. Because the students did not enjoy the pedagogy of the general group work applied in the class, they were negative about the Social Group Therapeutic Group work technique that formed the focus of the module. The module covers the basic theory and practice of social group work as one of the three primary methods (casework, group work, and community work) that social workers use. The aim of the module is intended to provide learners with a basic and foundation knowledge and understanding of social group work skills and principles. The rationale of the module is to introduce students to various aspects of social group work dynamics and processes, including stages of social group work theory, decision making, formulation of a group, as well as understanding how group work "fits in" to contemporary social work practice in a South African context. Thus, although the focus of the module is on psycho-educational group work, which is treatment-orientated in social work, the pedagogy of TBL can be implemented from a general educational approach so that challenges that the lecturer and students experience with the traditional approach to using group work in teaching and learning may be addressed. Also, through successful TBL, students can share, support, guide and encourage each other as they function in a group. It may be that through these TBL activities social networks can form that will help students address the challenges they face to achieve success.

Team-Based Learning

The Principles of Team-Based Learning

TBL is a well-established and systematic approach to group work that integrates individual study out of class, immediate feedback out of class and in-class and small-group activities in class to create an engaging learning environment, supported and evaluated by peers (Cohen & Robinson, 2018). One of the outcomes of applying TBL is increased student performance (Goodson, 2004). This is based on the principle of student engagement (or active learning) (Michaelsen & Sweet, 2008) during group work, resulting in deeper learning. Active-learning strategies enable students to become more actively involved in course content and promoting student learning experiences. In figure 1, the effect of active learning activities on student learning as explained by Krivickas (2005) is presented.

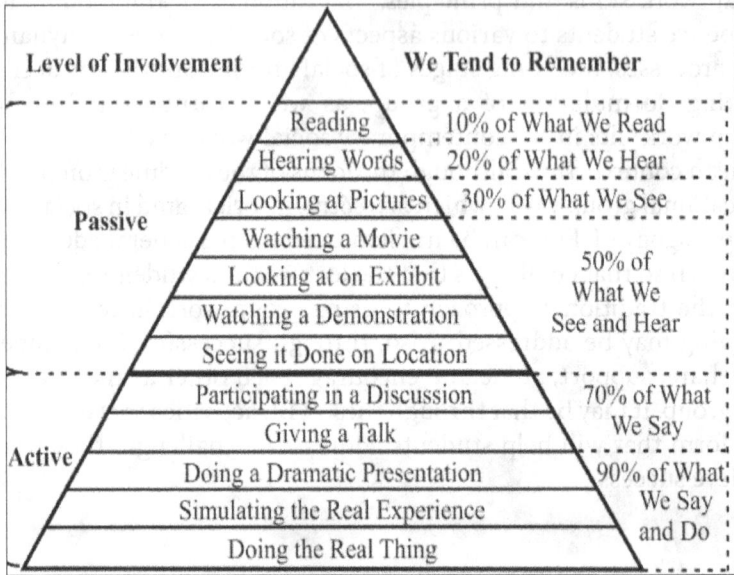

Figure 1: The cone of learning (Krivickas, 2005)

The more actively students engage in collaborative learning (e.g. discussions, talks, presentations, simulation, real experience), the more they will remember what they learn (deeper learning). According to Chin and Brown (2000) typical student actions related to surface learning is when they give explanations that are reformulations of the questions that are asked in the class, or descriptions of objects which referred only to what was visible in class. On the other hand, Chin and Brown (2000) further explains that students use a deep learning approach when they venture their ideas more spontaneously; give more elaborate explanations which described mechanisms and cause-effect relationships or referred to personal experiences; asked questions which focused on explanations and causes, predictions, or resolving discrepancies in knowledge. This will typically happen in cooperative learning activities during TBL. Seif (2018) motivates the importance of deep learning by explaining that it helps develop students' knowledge, abilities, and competencies necessary for living, working and good citizenship in a 21st-century world. Deep learning promotes the qualities students need for success by building complex understanding and meaning rather than focusing on the learning of superficial knowledge that can today be gleaned through search engines. "Deep learning instruction provides students with the advanced skills necessary to deal with a world in which good jobs are becoming more cognitively demanding. It prepares them to be curious, continuous, independent learners as well as thoughtful, productive, active citizens in a democratic society" (Seif, 2018:online).

Application of TBL

One of the crucial elements for successful TBL is the formation of the teams. Sibley et al. (2014) explain that TBL teams need to be large enough to provide intellectual power to the groups, thus 5–6 members per team is recommended. Teams should also be created by the lecturer, and not by the students. Student-selected teams are what Sibley et al. (2014:9) call "social entities" that underperform and that do not form the same cohesion as teacher-formed teams. The third element of successful TBL is the diversity of the teams. Sibley et al. (2014) explain that heterogeneity in teams ensures that a wide range of skills, opinions, and personal experiences come to play during team discussions and problem-solving. This is especially important for social learning, as diverse teams provide a rich source of students' experiences, perceptions, advice, and knowledge that the students can share. It is also through these diverse teams that students can form new social networks for additional support outside of the classroom. Goodson (2004:123) found that one of the outcomes of implementing TBL in her class was her students "making friends and learning how to work in groups."

The TBL class does not include a formal, comprehensive, theoretical lesson as in traditional lectures. This implies that all the theories that apply to a specific scheduled class must be studied and understood before the students engage in active learning during contact sessions. Students must understand basic theoretical concepts and ideas to contribute to the class exercise and to complete it (Eksteen et al., 2018).

According to Sibley et al. (2014) TBL is applied in five phases (Figure 2):

Phase 1: Before the contact session, students receive preparatory materials for pre-reading and studying of basic concepts and ideas relevant to the scheduled class. Students have to complete a reading quiz, the Readiness Assurance Preparation (RAP) as a form of promoting individual accountability and to help students prepare for the social learning that will take place in the class. These reading assignments include textbooks, articles or lecture notes. In the Social work module, the students receive reading assignments on their Learning Management System (LMS) to prepare for the next contact session. A short multiple-choice test on the assigned reading is included on the LMS for the students to complete before the next contact session.

Phase 2: During the contact session, at the beginning of the class, students complete an individual readiness assurance test (iRAT), to confirm their understanding of the theory. Because the social work class was small enough, short questions were asked on the relevant theory. This can be alternated with multiple-choice questions if needed.

Phase 3: This is then followed by a Team Readiness Assurance Test (tRAT) where the same test is retaken by the team. The social work teams had the opportunity to retake the test, but before completing the test, they could discuss the possible answers in the team before deciding on one answer for the whole team. This is a form of team teaching and collaborative learning that provided support to those students who struggled with the work.

Phase 4: Students are then encouraged to ask questions or clarify answers on which they did not agree during a process known as the Appeals Process. In the social work class, the teams exchanged their tests with another group for peer marking. This provided an opportunity for students to ask questions regarding the answers, to clarify the work and to debate about the possible answers.

Phase 5: This is followed by a short mini lecture on unclear topics or areas that the students still feel uncertain about. The social work lecturer prepared a short PowerPoint lecture in which the main topics were revised to provide yet another opportunity of learning.

The remaining class time is then allocated to the application of the module concepts, in exercises designed to give the students a deeper understanding of the module and to get an in-depth view of the content. These application-oriented team exercises of give-and-take discussions help promote problem-solving, co-operation and critical thinking (Michaelen et al., 2008). The social work lecturer provided authentic scenarios on therapeutic treatment groups which the different teams had to discuss and then complete three questions, e.g. how the theory was applied in these scenarios, how they would apply the theory, and what recommendations will they make to social workers regarding similar therapeutic treatment group work scenarios. The last part of the contact session is then used for the different teams to give feedback to the class as a whole on the three questions so that everybody gets a complete overview of the work, and they can gain different perspectives on the work.

During phases 1 and 2, the focus is on individual learning. It can be during this stage that students may struggle with the content on their own, resulting in anxiety and lack of confidence. During Phases 3–5, the value of TBL becomes relevant as students engage in discussions, explaining the work to each other, receive support from their peers and confirm their understanding of the content. It is during these group work sessions that social learning takes place.

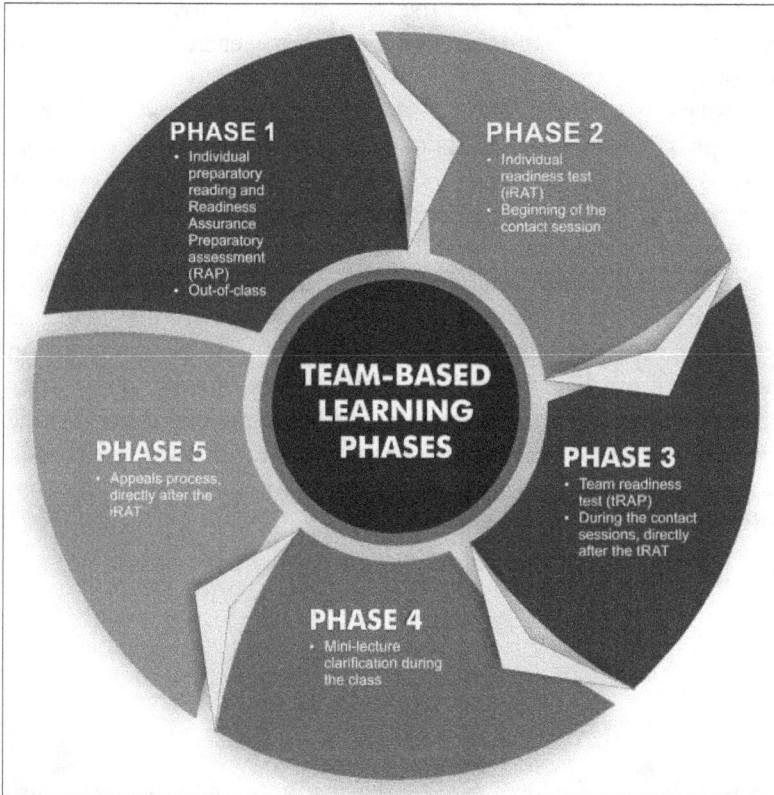

Figure 2: The Team-Based Learning phases (Adapted from Sibley et al., 2014).

Conclusion

Universities have implemented processes and programmes to provide access to students who were previously not able to attend higher education institutes. These students face several challenges based on their background and the unfamiliar university context. Although some support programmes are in place, e.g. dedicated student support divisions and financial support, students still struggle to cope in the learning environment. These students need support in the classroom in the form of social networking and peer support. By creating an environment where students can learn with each other and from each other, the chances for these students to survive and thrive in a university setting increases. A pedagogy that supports active learning in groups is TBL. Team-Based Learning is a well-researched approach to effective group work in classes and is successfully implemented in a variety of disciplines. Lecturers should follow the five distinct phases of TBL for effective implementation. The advantage of implementing TBL in a social work module is that students learn how to work in groups effectively, and how to apply group work techniques in practice – skills that are especially important for social work. An additional advantage of implementing TBL is the collaborative and supportive environment that it creates in class. Students guide and support each other to complete tasks, thus creating an environment where students who experience challenges in other environments can function and achieve their learning goals.

References

Cele, N. & Menon, K. (2006). Social exclusion, access and the restructuring of higher education in South Africa. *South African Journal of Higher Education, 20*(3), 38–50.

Chin, C. & Brown, D. E. (2000). Learning in Science: A comparison of deep and surface approaches. *Journal of Research in Science Teaching, 37*(2), 109–138, doi:10.1002/(SICI)1098-2736(200002)37:2<109: AID-TEA3>3.0.CO;2-7

Cohen, J. & Robinson, C. (2018). Enhancing teaching excellence through team-based learning. *Innovations in Education and Teaching International, 55*(2),133–142, doi:10.1080/12403297.2017.1389290

Cross, M. & Carpentier, C. (2009). "New students" in South African higher education: institutional culture, student performance and the challenge of democratization. *Perspectives in Education, 27*(1), 6–18.

Eksteen, M. J., Reitsma, G. M., Swart, S. B., & Fourie, E. (2018). Team-based learning experiences of fourth-year pharmacy students in a South African University. *American Journal of Pharmaceutical Education, 82*(1), 41–49.

Ezhumalai, S., Muralidhar, D., Dhanasekarapandian, R., & Nikketha, B. S. (2018). Group interventions. *Indian Journal of Psychiatry, 60*(Suppl 4), 514–521, doi:10.4203/psychiatry.IndianJPsychiatry_42_18

Goodson, P. (2004). Working with non-traditional and underprepared students in health education. In Michaelsen, L. K., Bauman Knight, A., & Findk, L. D. (Eds.), *Team-based learning. A transformative use of small groups in college teaching* (pp. 115–123) Virginia. USA: Stylus.

Jacobs, M., Vakalisa, N. C. G., & Gawe, N. (2011). *Teaching learning dynamics.* Cape Town, SA: Heinemann/Pearson.

Johnson, D. W. & Johnson, R. T. (2009). An educational psychology success story: Social interdependence theory and cooperative learning. *Educational Researcher, 38*(5), 365–379, doi:10.3102/0013189X09339057

Krivickas, R. (2005). Active learning at Kaunas University of Technology. *Global Journal of Engineering Education, 9*(1), 43–38.

Laal, M. & Ghodsi, S. M. (2012). Benefits of collaborative learning. *Procedia – Social and Behavioural Sciences, 31*, 486–490. doi:10.1016/j.sbspro.2100.12.091

Michaelsen, L. K. & Sweet, M. (2008). The essential elements of team-based learning. *New directions for teaching and learning, 116*, 7–27.

Mills, M. & McGregor, G. (2013). *Re-engaging young people in education.* eBook London: Routledge. doi:https://doi.org/10.4324/9781315880433

Penn, S. (2017). *Five basic elements of cooperative learning.* Retrieved from http://tutorials.istudy.psu.edu/cooperativelearning/cooperativelearning4.html

Ross, E. (2010). Selection tests and social justice: a profile of applicants seeking admission to the social work undergraduate degree at a South African University. *Social work education, 29*(5), 459–474. doi:10.1080/2615470903177630

Sands, R. G. & Solomon, P. (2003). Developing educational groups in social work practice. *Social work with groups. 26*(2), 5–21. doi:10.1300/J009v26n02_02

Scager, K., Boonstra, J., Peeters, T., & Wiegant, F. (2016). Collaborative learning in Higher Education: Evoking positive interdependence. *CBE life sciences education 15*(4), 1–9, doi: 10.1187/cbe.16-07-0219

Seif, E. (2018). What is deep learning? Who are the deep learning teachers? *ASCD In-Service.* Retrieved from https://inservice.ascd.org/what-is-deep-learning-who-are-the-deep-learning-teachers/

Sennet, J., Finchilescu, G., Gibson, K., & Strauss, R. (2003). Adjustment of Black Students at a historically White South African University. *Educational Psychology, 23*(10), 107–116.

Sibley, J., Ostafichuk, P., Roberson, B., Franchini, B., & Kubitz, K. A. (2014). *Getting started with Team-Based Learning.* Stylus: Sterling Virginia, USA.

Snyder, J. J., Sloane, J. D., Dunk. R. D., & Wiles, J. R. (2016). Peer-led team learning helps minority students succeed. *PLoS Biol, 14*(3), e1002398, https://doi.org/10.1371/journal.pbio.1002398

Social justice education, 3Rs. (2019). *Social justice education. Online Inservice.* Retrieved from https://rrr.edu.au/unit/module-1/topic-3/social-justice/

Terenzini, P. T., Cavrera, A. F., Colbeck, C. L., Parente, J. M., & Bjorklund. S. A. (2001). Collaborative learning vs lecture/discussion: students' reported learning gains. *Journal of Engineering Education, 90*(1), 123–130. https://doi.org/10.1002/j.2168-9830.2001.tb00579.x

Wiese, M., Botha, E., & van Heerden, G. (2015). Social relations beyond Team-Based Learning. In: K. Kubacki (Eds.) *Ideas in marketing: Finding the new and polishing the old. Developments in marketing science: Proceedings of the Academy of Marketing Science.* (pp. 331–334) Springer, Cham.

Wilson-Delfosse, A. L. (2012). Team-based learning: From educational theory to emotional intelligence. *Medical Teacher, 34*(10), 781–782.

Methodology for understanding human behaviors in a social environment

Mamadou M. Seck

Introduction

Long after the independence of some African countries, social work educators designed a new profile for social workers since they recognized the status of social workers as change agents for community development. The introduction of the Rapid Rural Participatory Research Methodology (RPRM) in schools of social work curricula was the consequence of a paradigm shift. These educators, along with most African post-colonial administrators, found out that many projects designed by the already-established European expertise did not meet residents' expectations. Further, they faced the evidence that many of the responses these experts put in place to solve local communities' problems were neither effective nor efficient. Consequently, as public and private sectors' administrators decided to solicit more local expertise to develop community programs, social work school administrators opted to include the RPRM in their schools' curriculum. They deemed that this training would not only enhance the quality of social work students' expertise, hence opening employment opportunities for new graduates, but would also help meet the needs of local development programs.

Ideally, an inter-professional or multidisciplinary team conducts the RPRM as an evaluative intervention strategy. Members of the team should be of different backgrounds including social workers, sociologists, doctors, nurses, veterinarians, teachers, and other specialties. Based on their field of expertise, they contribute to the process and content of the group work. For example, a medical doctor or nurse would be focusing on identifying the various diseases that plague the residents and the needed treatments and medication. Another group member whose specialty is agricultural engineering would look into the quality of the soil, the adequate technology for farming, and the needed equipment for improving the quality and quantity of the farming production. Consequently, based on group members' specialties, a series of specific activities, and tools and techniques enable researchers to assess the potentials of a village in various domains. Originally, the RPRM has been designed to be used in rural areas but, due to its efficiency and flexibility, it has been used in assessing programs and several activities in urban and semi-urban areas. Following the description of the two phases of the training, the students' knowledge and skills earned as well as the implications for practice, advocacy, and policy, are discussed.

The phases of a Rapid Participatory Research Methodology training

One lead-faculty instructor with a long practice experience running RPRM workshops is assigned to work with a team of trainers including other faculty members and graduate teaching assistants. These instructors intervene during the introductory workshop phase that takes place in the school as well as during the field practice session in the villages as many of them either teach specific sections of the curriculum or supervise students when they complete their field activities.

The Introductory Workshop Phase

Early in the semester, long before the training, a team of faculty members completes a prospection operation that consists of visiting several prospective sites where the field practice may take place. These visits enable them to learn more about the sites, the location, and the main issues and social problems residents face. After these field prosecutions, the instructors return to the school to decide which villages will be targeted for the studies and accordingly prepare their lectures for the workshop.

During a five-day introductory phase, students attend a workshop aimed at preparing them to implement the RPRM and to master its process, tools, and techniques. The objectives of the workshop are as follows: After attending this workshop, participants will

- Be able to work in groups as effective participants in group activities.
- Be able to create a new relationship and socialize with residents.
- Be able to run focus groups and individual interviews to collect and analyze data.
- Be able to draw and interpret village maps, tables, diagrams, and charts.
- Be able to write a complete field report.

To reach the workshop objectives, faculty members introduce students to the use of various field investigation tools and data collection strategies as, once in the field, they have to collect and analyze data such as historical events that took place in the village, community needs, and the location and use of natural resources like water, soil, and plants. The instruments they use vary and include the village's history and map, a Venn diagram that shows the various local organizations, a seasonal calendar, and needs pyramids. For example, after a guided tour around the village, students draw a map of the site in collaboration with few residents to ascertain its authenticity. On the map, they have to indicate the locations of the main buildings, the landscape, roads, dirt paths between farms for traveling cattle, and natural resources sites. After identifying all the existing associations created by the residents, students draw Venn diagrams to show how connected these groups are. Usually, they draw a large circle that represents the village and within the circle, several overlapping, connected, or separated small circles are drawn to represent these local organizations. When two associations share membership, they intersect to show their connections. If well done, this instrument may reveal unsuspected relationships between local, national, and international entities (see Fig: 1–Venn diagram). The activities of those organizations may be revealed on a seasonal calendar which is an instrument that illustrates the consecutive periods of the year when agricultural activities such as planting, harvesting, and commercializing the crops occur.

Students are prepared to run focus groups during the training session. In fact, before going to the villages, they are offered the opportunity to review the theory relevant to running focus groups that they have already learned in class and then, they observe and

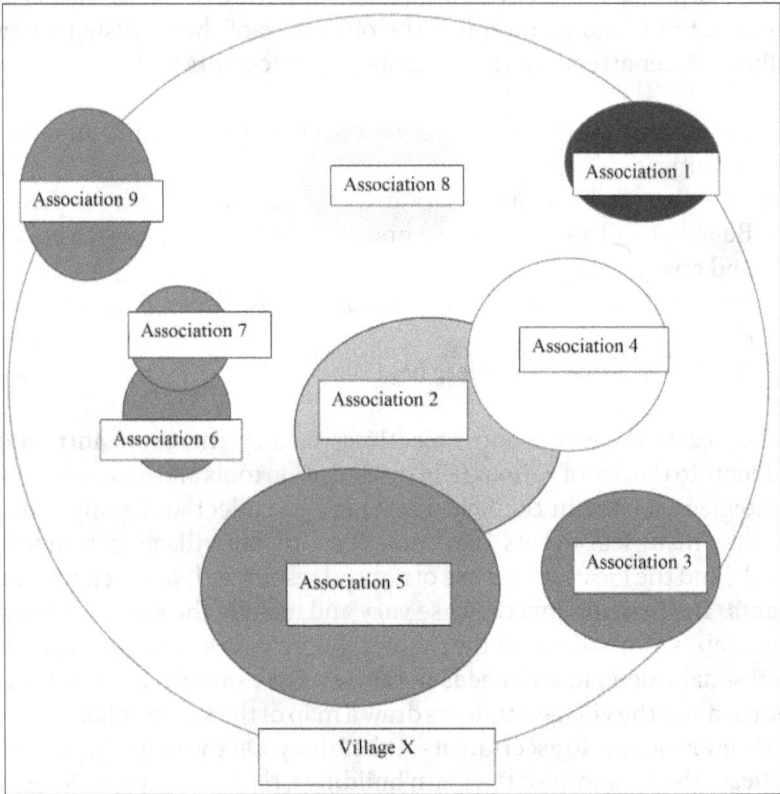

Figure 1. Venn diagram

participate in mock focus group sessions. While in the villages, they must demonstrate their skills in running focus groups with various components of the population, women, men, boys, and girls, since needs vary from one group to another. For example, to identify the needs of local populations, students may interview groups of female or male participants only or groups of children only. For example, they may initiate one needs assessment for women using one semi-structured instrument with the following two open-ended questions:

- What are the main problems facing you now in this village?
- What do you need right now that would alleviate your life in this village?

Participants' responses to these two main questions may lead the interviewers to ask many subsequent questions such as:

- Which problem needs to be solved first?
- What actions should the government implement to solve the problems?
- What can you do to solve these problems?

Since participants' responses may lead to many more follow-up questions, the interview may last hours. Once it is completed, the students draw pyramids that reflect a prioritization of the stated needs from the most urgent one at the base to the least urgent one at the top of the pyramid. Each pyramid is drawn as a bar chart with each bar representing one identified specific need (see Figure 2: Women pyramid of needs). Because of the specificity of the needs of women, men, and children, usually, at least three pyramids are drawn representing the needs of each group. These pyramids may reveal several problems facing the village that ought to be solved. Students may refer to these results to draw another instrument "a problem-tree" of the village with the roots representing the factors causing the problems, the trunk being the main problems, and the branches and leaves depicting the consequences of the problems.

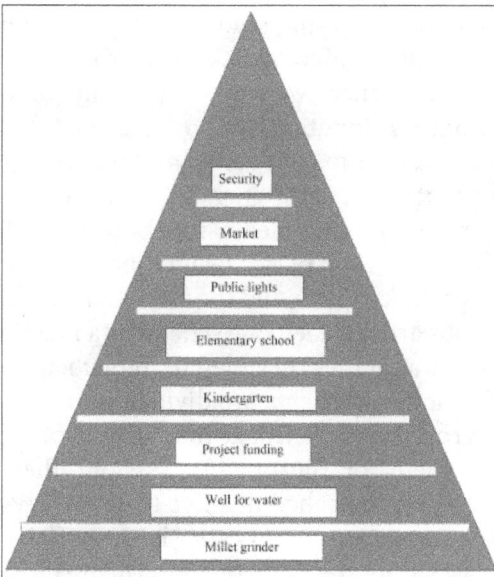

Figure 2. Women pyramid of needs

The variety of tools and the village residents' collaboration empowers students to be successful in collecting information with the most common data collection methods including the focus groups, the individual and collective interviews, and field visits. To validate the results of the interviews, a triangulation session takes place. For example, the women who participated in the needs assessment are invited to review the pyramids that the researchers drew so they can express their agreement or disagreement on the ranking of their needs as listed on the drawing. This session entitled "restitution phase" is an opportunity to empower women to validate or reject the research findings as they have the power to confirm or contest the ranking of the needs as presented on the pyramid. If they reject the researchers' prioritization of the expressed needs, they are asked to complete their ranking of the findings.

Field practice phase

Before the workshop ends, the instructors' team meets and determines the criteria for assigning students to the various groups. As they have been supervising and educating students, they have an idea of their abilities, and strengths and weaknesses; so they use these criteria as well as their experience working with them to complete these assignments. Students' input may also be considered. Among the selection criteria, leadership, and verbal and written communication skills are listed. Other criteria such as "ease to work with," and "reliability in completing assignments" may be used. Each group is then placed under the supervision of two faculty members, one playing the role of the principal investigator and the other that of a field supervisor. Once all the groups are set, each one schedules a meeting to establish the timetable of the activities they plan to implement in the field.

For the field practice, students are divided into groups of 10 to 15 members. Each group joins the village that the school's administration had assigned to them for the practice session. They stay in their designated villages for the scheduled five to seven days the program lasts. Each day, the group selects its "leader of the day" who is responsible for assigning the daily tasks to the members and defines their roles. As these leaders manage any conflict within the groups, they are assisted by the two instructors who support them in maintaining their group cohesion and setting up the schedule, so all activities are completed in time.

Dwelling on-site provides students the opportunity to experience residents' living conditions. Before they arrive in the village, the chief and council members had decided to assign to the group a few huts, barracks, or other places to stay like those of residents. The students take advantage of their stay to apply the research techniques they learned earlier during the workshop. They are exposed to concrete situations that they need to assess and learn from according to the daily schedule they agreed upon. With the supervising team, they identify and integrate various local committees to implement research activities that require them to be embedded within local groups. Several village residents are selected to be part of the research teams as research informants, guides, and consultants. Usually, they are selected based on the recommendation of the village chief and council members following a meeting with the principal investigator and field supervisor who informs them about the profile of the persons they are looking for. Along with the students, these selected villagers participate in most data collection activities such as the focus groups, and semi-structured interviews. Further, when interviews are conducted with local groups, specific organizations, and individuals, they may have to translate or clarify the interviewees' responses as well as the interviewers' questions. In many circumstances, the fact that students speak the same language the villagers use facilitates these exchanges; also, French is usually a shared common language.

Daily meetings are held for data analysis, brainstorming, planning activities, and writing sections of the report. All the phases of group development, pre-group planning, beginning, middle, and ending can be observed. For example, the various activities for the day are discussed during the pre-group planning. During the beginning phase, the new members are introduced to the larger group. Also, the purpose of the activities as well as the roles, norms, and rules are established. During the middle phase or the working stage, an effective communication process facilitates data collection and sharing. Finally, a report on the activities illustrates the ending phase. The group decision-making process, leadership, power, boundaries, conflicts, and productivity are among the many issues studied as students are exposed to these phenomena. At the end of the training, the village residents are invited to participate in triangulation sessions to discuss and verify the credibility and dependability of the research findings. The writing and submission of the report occur only after these triangulation sessions. Later, faculty members grade the reports and then send revised copies to the Ministry of Families and Social Services. Nonprofit organizations may have access to them as they look for villages where they may intervene. The government, as well as nonprofit organizations, may refer to the reports when they plan to initiate and implement development projects that may impact the future of the villages and enhance the quality of life of the residents.

Discussions and implications

Identifying and addressing clients' needs and potentials in the physical and social environment they live in requires that social workers know and understand the challenges these individuals face due to their conditions. Therefore, teaching social workers how to get involved in research activities and apply the adequate methodology is among the main objectives of social work education which promotes specifically evidence-based research. The introduction of the RPRM in West African schools of social work curricula aimed at meeting this objective. This training described above has been designed to provide social work students with opportunities to gain knowledge and skills that enable them to meet their professional objectives since they are expected to effectively and efficiently assess rural populations' needs, potentials, and interactions with the environment. This research methodology has been part of the curriculum of social work schools in West Africa, particularly in Francophone institutions where it is known as "Méthodologie accélérée de Recherche participative" (Gueye & Freudenberger, 1991). Variations of this RPRM are known as "Rapid Rural Appraisals" (Chambers, 1994), "Action Research" (Cordeiro & Soares, 2016; Keegan, 2016; Santos, Ali, & Hill, 2016; Tavares, 2016), "Community Based Research" in the United States. Its inclusion in the curriculum not only seems to have enhanced social work students' potential for employment due to the quality of their knowledge and skills in practice, advocacy and policy, and research.

What do students learn? What are the implications for practice, advocacy and policy, and research?

The training which includes both the in-school introductory workshop and field practicum in a village offers students an opportunity to apply what they already learned in group work, the principles and processes, stages of group development, group cohesion, and evaluation of members' interactions, leadership, conflicts, and problem-solving. Further, it aims to enhance their skills in time management and task completion when involved in community development interventions. Consequently, students' integration of the objectives of the training has various implications for practice, advocacy and policy, and research.

Implication for practice

During the field practice, students integrate various local groups, associations, teams, committees, and possibly boards of local agencies. They are offered opportunities to apply their knowledge in group process and content as they are exposed to various group structures and phenomena. Interviewing villagers may require them to draw and use Venn diagrams to identify groups that share membership, space, and objectives. These diagrams help them acquire a good understanding of the social and commercial interrelations within one village and between various rural communities. They may also reveal unexpected exchange trends between villages, nearby cities, and even foreign countries. Also, they may facilitate verbal communications between researchers and villagers since many of the participants, despite their illiteracy, are knowledgeable about the conditions they live in and the problems they face. It is important to stress that they may be illiterate in French but proficient in other languages such as Arabic because many of them may have attended Islamic schools, so they can write and speak Arabic in addition to their native language.

In the context of developing countries, gaining knowledge on rural populations' needs and living conditions strengthens social workers' understanding of phenomena such as the rural exodus that afflicts local communities and the strenuous relationship between sedentary farmers and nomadic shepherds. Consequently, instructors' roles include helping students sharpen their skills in designing programs for not only men and women who leave their villages to migrate to cities to find work but also to support them so they can manage their activities while staying in cities. Further, the faculty members are expected to help students develop conflict management skills so they not only can help farmers and herders develop and maintain positive relationships but also facilitate effective dialogues and maintain open channels of communication between these two communities with very different lifestyles. Due to these skills, social workers are among the most designated practitioners when it comes to bringing farmers and herders to collaborate as they discuss and map out the dirt paths allowing cattle to move through farms without damage. Their interventions, therefore, are necessary to avoid conflicts between the two communities.

Implications for advocacy and policy

Students' knowledge of the implications of policies in local, national, and international arena enables them to develop skills in designing and implementing social action strategies aimed at preventing social problems and enhancing the quality of life in rural areas. Further, as they are aware of government regulations' impact on local businesses and nonprofit organizations, they are prepared to be able to raise residents' awareness of their rights and obligations, and possibly motivate them to get involved in civic actions and self-advocacy. They are also able to empower villagers themselves to define the problems they face and determine their way to solve them. Further, they may develop leadership skills in gathering information and collaborating with public officials and legislators to raise their awareness of emerging social problems and engage the latter to find solutions that satisfy villagers.

Implications for research

As social program designers, students develop and apply skills in need assessment activities. For example, in each village, one of their tasks is to assess the needs of women, men, and youth. Completing a needs assessment may prompt them not only to initiate social programs aiming at improving the welfare and wellbeing of the residents but also to evaluate existing local programs. Further, students are exposed to the exchanges of goods, products, and services that take place between the villages they study and neighboring communities. They are offered the opportunity to draw charts that illustrate residents' migration flows as well as the inter-relations between the villages. Further, because they know that people's lives are intertwined with their social environment, they can discuss and analyze the impact of the social context on the residents' relationships as well as the constraints facing men, women, and children. This skill is necessary when they make proposals aiming to bridge the divide between communities.

One of the most important phases of the field practice is the validation of the research findings by the village residents. As researchers, students need to develop their skills in documenting reliable and valid findings. Therefore, practicing this triangulation phase of the study process strengthens their research abilities. They become more and more proficient in reaching credible and dependable results.

Conclusion

RPRM outcomes have been found effective in evaluating needs and helping create effective programs in rural areas. Meanwhile, these positive results have been reached following some revisions of the research processes. Several limitations have been identified on the design as well as on the utilization of the tools. In effect, some of the instruments such as the "aerial view of the region" and the "seasonal calendar" have been found difficult to use and at times very complex to analyze; in many cases, the groups' living conditions had been found extremely difficult for students and faculty members and consequently, several arrangements had to be made to improve these conditions so to facilitate their stay. Therefore, after more than a decade long application, and following some adjustments and corrections, the outcome of the RPRM training program illustrates the effective results of students' group work activities in research action and economic development. Despite its limitations, the RPRM has been maintained in social work schools' curricula and students' mastery of the methodology has proven to be a major factor in the hiring process of graduating cohorts since governments no longer automatically hire them in public positions. Its success is also a determinant reason for various African, European, and North American schools of social work to send their students to the Dakar School of Specialized Social Workers for field practicum so they can take advantage of the RPRM training. Further, it has contributed to bridging the divide between people within the same community but also between individuals and organizations from various communities, and countries.

References

Chambers, R. (1994). Participatory Rural Appraisal (PRA): Analysis of Experience. *World Development, 22*(9), 1253–1268.

Cordeiro, L. & Soares, C. B. (2016). Implementation of evidence-based health care using action research: An emancipatory approach. *International Journal of Nursing Practice, 22*, 333–338.

Gueye, B. & Freudenberger, K. S. (1991). Introduction a la Méthode Accélérée De Recherche Participative (MARP). Rapid Rural Appraisal; Quelques Notes Pour Appuyer Une Formation Pratique. (2nd Ed.). International Institute for Environment and Development, London.

Keegan, R. (2016). Action Research as an Agent for Enhancing Teaching and Learning in Physical Education: A Physical Education Teacher's Perspective. *The Physical Educator, 73*, 255–284.

Santos, I. M., Ali, N., & Hill, A. (2016). Students as Co-designers of a Virtual Learning Commons: Results of a Collaborative Action Research Study. *The Journal of Academic Librarianship, 42*, 8–14.

Tavares, C. (2016). Human rights education and the research process: action research as a tool for reflection and change. *Educational Action Research, 24*(4), 617–634.

Rediscovering the power of group work in promoting social justice for older persons

Leanne Jordaan

Introduction

Upholding a socially just society requires agile, responsive social work services. It is therefore imperative that social workers not only remain consistently aware of which vulnerable groups require involvement, but that social work training and education adequately equip professionals to meet these needs.

There is a sense of urgency developing in the field of social work to ensure that one of the most rapidly increasing marginalised groups, that of older persons, receives the attention it deserves before we run the risk of neglecting our responsibility as social workers in upholding and protecting justice in society. In the context of being a practice educator, this translates into incorporating programmes which ensure that students are not only educated to understand societal needs but are equipped to work in practice in addressing these needs and demands. Currently, on the international and national levels, there is an increasing need for social workers to be trained to work with older persons, as the rise in elderly people continues (DuBois & Miley, 2014).

Working as a practice educator in a dual position at a university and being affiliated to a family-based Non-Government Organisation (NGO), offers me the opportunity to combine educational requirements with practice-based needs. Final year social work students, as part of fulfilling their practice related requirements for their degree, are placed at organisations for practice work experience, of which the mentioned organisation is such a placement.

The opportunity for working with older persons is offered at the placement where students are encouraged to develop their skills in this field. It was noticed, however, that students expressed resistance in working with older persons. This is not a new phenomenon and literature reflecting student resistance or negative attitudes toward older persons is widely documented (Fraboni et al., 1990; Kalavar, 2001; Rupp et al., 2005 in Allan & Johnson, 2008). More specifically, social work student resistance in working with older persons was documented two decades ago, in an article shared by Quinn (2000) which recognised a similar general lack of interest and reluctance as we continue to observe.

Group work, through the facilitation of community-based task groups, can offer a solution that not only provides a necessary and relevant approach to working with older persons but also addresses students' resistance to working with this population.

This paper aims to share the numerous benefits identified in using community-based groups with older persons, as the central focus of a programme designed by and for the community. To support this claim, a practice example of a student-facilitated group work intervention, within a South African residential care facility, with its intended and unintended outcomes will be discussed.

In the discussion of the practice example, the achievement of various outcomes will be addressed, including the dual achievement of increasing the motivation and commitment of both the students and older persons to the intervention process. The significant changes in the profile of older persons, including how policies have been developed to respond to the changes will also be highlighted. The role of group work, in working with older persons, also receives attention to contextualise its applicability in the practice example. Group work has a role to play in ensuring relevant service delivery to older persons and can also be considered a useful method in enhancing students' interest to work in this field. Using group work, as discussed in the practice example, reflects the power of group work to remain a part of the journey in ensuring social justice for older persons.

Older persons and the role of group work in service delivery

An essential starting point in working with older persons is to recognise the changes in the profile of this group in society. The updated profile of older persons firstly shows that there is a vast increase in numbers and underlines how the traditional view of working with older persons as passive recipients has become replaced by the dynamic principles found in the World Health Organisation (WHO) World Report on Ageing and Health (2015).

Population ageing, referred to by Bloom, Mitgang and Osher (2016) as the "dominant demographic trend of this century" indicates that longevity is increasing, and the percentage and number of older persons are higher than ever before. The United Nations Population Division (UN, 2017) predicts an increase in the number of older persons (aged 60 years+) from 962 million in 2017, to more than twice that number by 2050, a projection of nearly 2.1 billion older persons. Pretorius (2019) sees population ageing as becoming one of the most significant social transformations of this century, which will have an unavoidable impact on all sectors in society.

As the size of the group increases, so too, the stereotypes and generalisations regarding older persons seem to increase. It is generally assumed that older persons have similar traits and characteristics. However, research shows that this group is more heterogeneous than any other age group and that the older we get, the more dissimilar we are. Older persons continue to be seen as rigid and unable to change; however, people continuously change throughout their life span. The actual age factor is seen to be a less important indicator of flexibility than a person's attitude towards aging (DuBois & Miley, 2019; Moses, 2012).

In the South African context, the response to the changes in society, with specific reference to older persons, is reflected in the changes in legislation and policy. Goodrick (2013) provides an outline of these developments which include:

1974: The South African government started working on active population policy programmes, which included the 1974 Family Planning Programme.

1984: The Population Development Programme (PDP) was

implemented to address the lowering of a rapidly growing population.

1998: The National Population Policy for South Africa was developed to adjust and align policies with international frameworks.

2005: The South Africa National Plan of Action for Older Persons was developed and focused on achieving the three key areas of the International Madrid Plan of Action on Ageing (2002).

2006: The Older Persons Act 13 of 2006 was developed which included strategies on how to meet the relevant needs of the growing elderly population.

2008: The review of the 1990 Population Policy indicated an acknowledgment of population ageing as a concern of the South African population.

Noticeable is the integration of international and national frameworks which recognise the increase in the numbers of older persons in society as well as the incorporation of ways in which to address the needs of the group while maintaining dignity and growth. A repeated theme is that older persons want to actively participate and contribute to their world in a dignified and worthwhile manner. Contributing to society forms the underpinning of social justice which recognises the mutual interdependence of persons and community, and stresses participation as both the duty of individuals and responsibility of society (Moses, 2012).

Healthy Ageing is the focus of WHO's work on ageing between 2015–2030, and replaces the World Health Organization's 2002 Active Ageing: a policy framework, which defines Healthy Ageing as "the process of developing and maintaining the functional ability that enables well-being in older age" (WHO, 2015:28). Healthy Ageing, like Active Ageing, emphasizes the need for action across multiple sectors and enabling older people to remain a resource to their families, communities, and economies.

Social workers are equipped as agents to facilitate and maintain dignified integration into communities and respect for the unique value of every human being, regardless of individual differences, cultural variations, or contributions to age (DuBois & Miley, 2014). Aligned to this view is the national Older Persons Act 13 of 2006 which is "intended to protect, promote and maintain the status, rights, well-being and security of older persons" (Department of Justice and Constitutional Development, 2019) and confirms the paramount role of social workers in work with older persons.

A current challenge in upholding the rights of older persons is the existence of ageism and age discrimination. Ageism refers to prejudicial attitudes about older persons and is in direct contravention to basic human rights, which are defined by DuBois and Miley (2014:133) as "the fundamental entitlements that are necessary for personal development and human potential." The impact of ageism has far-reaching effects. Ageism reduces the ability of older persons to contribute to communities, which is recognised as an essential part of active aging (DuBois & Miley, 2014). Furthermore, ageism perpetuates social exclusion and in combination with inadequate service delivery, results in high levels of old-age exclusion and the failure to address the needs of this specific group (Walsh, Scharf & Keating, 2016).

The role of group work in interventions with older persons

The message is established that the rapidly growing group of older persons, as a high-risk group in society, requires adequate and appropriate service delivery with a focus on ensuring that their need to contribute in society, is facilitated. Prinsloo (2015) correctly recognises that the responsibility to deliver the necessary services to older persons is shared by governmental, private, and religious organisations and that these entities must contribute to the older persons' well-being. The obvious question to follow relates to "how" to appropriately deliver services in work with older persons. "Starting where the client is" is a basic tenet of the social work profession (Birkenmaier & Berg-Weger, 2017). Ensuring effective service delivery when working with older persons, therefore, requires an understanding of the different elements and demands of this group. Changes in the older persons' profile reflect a clear shift from a group of passive and inflexible individuals, to dynamic participants who actively engage in their world.

The use of group work with older persons, with its many benefits, could provide the answer, as this intervention helps older persons to view their lives as meaningful (Prinsloo, 2015). Group work with older persons is seen to address challenges of aging and aids in combating social isolation and loneliness through providing social integration strategies (Corey et al., 2010; DuBois & Miley, 2019). In the article "Cutting and sewing brings Africa to the world: social justice for older people" Prinsloo (2019) provides an inspiring example of how group work with older persons enhances social justice through facilitating older persons' contributions to society. In the practice example to be discussed, specifically, the use and value of a community-based task group will be shared.

An important characteristic of a community-based task group is that it seeks not only to achieve the obvious goal of social change, but it places value on the role of the members and emphasizes member participation and contribution. The success of the group is directly linked to the level of member satisfaction and participation, and not only on whether the goal of the group was achieved or not (Staples, 2007).

Principles of the community-based task group reflect an understanding of the value of keeping group members involved and validate the importance of how members see themselves contributing. Group members' contributions are what drives the planned process, and this allows older persons to start contributing from the very beginning, until the end of the process. The function of organising in the task group is recognised as a bottom-up philosophical approach to activating social change through a collective action requiring "people power" for the achievement of goals (Staples, 2004). Older persons, the "people power" in the example, are therefore fulfilling a central need to contribute, through the task team itself, and the success of the social goal attainment.

Group work with older persons noticeably holds multiple advantages and forms the crux of the practice example discussion provided in this paper.

A practice example: An intergenerational skills-transfer programme

Social work students are required to implement group work interventions at placement organisations as an integral component of their studies. At the placement organisation, the SAVF (previously known as the Suid-Afrikaanse Vrouefederasie), final year social work students are offered the opportunity to work with older persons, which provides a unique opportunity for preparing enthusiastic, competent and well-informed social workers to work with this vulnerable group.

This practice example focuses on the group work experience of a social work student, placed at a residential care facility in Pretoria, Tshwane, South Africa. As previously mentioned, students are inclined to be resistant to work with older persons within the residential care facilities and are often dismissive of suggestions to be involved in the provided social work interventions. Consideration was given to what is recognised by the National Association of Social Work (NASW) as the core component of the mission of the Social work profession, that of achieving social justice. This includes achieving social justice in a multi-cultural society and asks that educators not only teach students to recognise cultural and social diversities but enable students to practice within these diverse environments, confirming the importance of addressing student resistance within the practice setting (Jani, Osteen & Shipe, 2016; Corey, Corey & Corey, 2010).

Increasing the students' awareness of the needs and vulnerabilities of older persons was, therefore, a starting point in the group work process, which assisted in minimising initial reluctance through the provision of essential knowledge.

A discussion of the group work facilitation and the subsequent project will include excerpts from the student's reflection provided after the completion of the intervention at the care facility. First and foremost, the student conducted a situational analysis within the care facility as part of the preparatory phase. She recognised that many residents had skills and talents which they wished to share, and which would also provide the opportunity for engagement with external sources. Acquiring this information led to the planning of an intergenerational skills-transfer programme, with a focus on enhancing the social integration of older persons in the community. After acceptance of the proposed programme by the relevant parties, the student followed a process of identifying residents who could participate.

The student suggested that the programme focus on a process whereby suited residents could partake in developing basic practical and life-skills of local orphaned and vulnerable children who resided at a safe care placement in the local community. The children in the placement are often deprived of exposure to the development and nurturing of basic life competencies. The social work student and carers from the safe care placement considered the relevant skills to be shared and the aspects identified for the programme included teaching the children basic cooking and sewing skills as well as exposing the children to creative work including art and knitting.

Subsequently, the residents who accepted the invitation to be a part of the project formed a task group. Facilitated by the student social worker, the task group started an ad hoc committee with the primary purpose of meeting the need for a collective, planned change in their social environment (Zastrow, 2010). The community-based task group met several times before the implementation of the skills-transfer project for planning and decision-making processes. Specific decisions included confirming which safe care placement the children would be invited from, as well as the number of children to be included in the project.

Explaining the South African context is relevant for understanding the initial resistance of the task group members when they realised that the children identified were black and that their first language was Sepedi or Sesotho. South Africa has eleven official languages, of which Sepedi and Sesotho are two. Although there are people who speak a large number of these eleven languages, most South Africans speak their first language (mother tongue) and English as their second language. The task group members' first language is Afrikaans and therefore both the members and the children would be challenged to speak in their second language, English. Additionally, these white, Afrikaans speaking older persons, despite the developing interracial understanding in a post-apartheid society, had not been part of the transition towards democracy in a practical sense and were confronted with their prejudices.

As part of addressing the members' resistance, the student took the members of the task group to the selected safe care placement for mutual introduction purposes. The student described the process as follows:

> I decided to take the whole team to the safety house for a greet and meet session. Thought I would preside over the meeting but all I did was introduce myself and greet, and to my surprise, the team and the children took over. Within minutes they connected, the team shared briefly their life stories and skills and why and how they are participating in the project.

The student noted that the natural affinity which developed in the meeting of the participants, adapted the initial plan of accommodating four children per task member, to six children, to allow for as many children as possible to attend the programme. Uncertainty experienced most possibly by all participants, was replaced with a genuine interest in partaking in the programme and saw the older persons eager to be involved in the children's lives.

After the initial meeting with the children, the task group met at frequent intervals for the planning and preparation of the skills transfer programme, which took place in the form of a one-week holiday programme, presented to the children at the older persons' residential care facility. The programme planning generated an enthusiastic atmosphere in the facility and saw increased participation as additional residents who were willing to partake in the skills-transfer programme, offered to join and share their skills. The task group members actively engaged in the required sourcing of funds and resources for the holiday programme.

During the implementation of the programme, each task group member facilitated their skills-transfer group with the selected children, providing primarily skills training in combination with varying additional activities, as mentioned by the student, such as motivational talks, singing and praying together and even teaching the children to play Bingo and Rummyikup. The student's involvement was minimal in the programme implementation phase, as the task group members actively took the leading role in the programme.

> *I must say that during that week, the team members facilitated their groups without any supervision and all I did was just to provide the resources and in some instances, they chased me away from the group because I was accused of being strict.*

The intergenerational skills-transfer programme ended with the children singing Afrikaans songs (the home language of most of the residents) to the entire group of residents in a gesture of appreciation for their involvement. As a surprise, the choirmaster had prepared the residents' choir to sing Sesotho hymns (the home language for most of the children) for the children.

The use of a task group consisting of older persons resulted in the implementation of an effective intergenerational skills-transfer programme. A discussion of the results of the practice example will be provided to reflect on the intended and unintended outcomes of the group work process and the programme in its entirety.

Discussion

The use of the community-based task group and the skills-transfer programme implemented in the residential care facility provides an example of how older persons can continue to contribute to society. The initial phase of the planning was driven primarily by the community-based task group and formed the basis of the programme. The involvement of the social work student gradually diminished from being actively involved in driving the process, to quietly witnessing the programme implementation. Various elements of the initial phases in the programme were driven by the task group and were deemed essential to its success. Firstly, the student was well informed, not only regarding the characteristics of older persons in general but through the situation analysis, of the specific needs of the residents in the facility. Secondly, the programme proposal was accepted by the residents and management of the facility and the mutual introduction of children and residents was a well-considered part of the process.

The practice example reflects a shift in views regarding working with older persons. Older persons are not seen as rigid and "already developed" but are in a process of continual development. The historic role and purpose of older persons in a society that focuses primarily on material and physical survival are neutralized as their need to contribute and engage in their communities is acknowledged and applied. The skills-transfer programme sought to include group members, with dignity, in their communities and broke the stigma of older persons as passive recipients of public aid. This, in turn, reflected a general shift from a needs-based, to a rights-based approach (DuBois & Miley, 2014, Moses, 2012:336; Goodrick, 2013).

The essential goal for achieving successful ageing as identified by the Macarthur Foundation Research Network on an Aging Society, of older persons' continuous engagement with life, including social relationships and productive activity, was achieved in the practice example (DuBois & Miley, 2014:414). The student shares this view:

During the preparation phase it dawned on me that the residents had a purpose, they had a voice, an agency, and control over their lives, and the groups they will be facilitating, and they also realised that they still have a chance to change the lives of others for the better.

Various goals, both intentional and unintentional, were achieved in addition to the promotion of active engagement and member participation. Sensitisation to a world, outside of the older persons' lives, yet an intricate part of their community, was developed by the task group members. The development of relationships between the older and the younger participants was significant. The older persons developed an understanding and appreciation for the orphaned and vulnerable children as they recognised similar signs of the impact of marginalisation in the lives of these children:

> *On our way back to the facility, the team couldn't stop talking about the children, the plans they had for them, the activities they have in mind, the food they will be cooking... What stood out for me was when Oom Johnny (a task team member) said "I will never feel sorry for myself or feel like I have nothing or I have been dumped, there are people out here who are suffering far more than us and have no hope for a better future."*

Relationships between the older persons and children started forming during their introduction and strengthened throughout the programme. Research confirms the mutual benefits of intergenerational programmes for both children and older persons. Studies show that older persons living in adult care facilities can experience social isolation which can lead to disenchantment, frustration, and depression; symptoms which can be alleviated through intergenerational programmes. Simultaneously, the lives of the children who engage with the older persons are enriched (Murayama et al., 2019). This form of intergenerational programme development by social workers is encouraged by Panda (2005) who asserts that children's attitudes towards older persons need to be addressed to instil respect and a sense of responsibility towards this group.

Also, a valuable contribution of the group and programme implementation included bridging both a racial and intergenerational divide. Reference has been made to the respectful gesture of both groups singing to each other in the others' mother tongue, a sign of cultural and racial acknowledgment and acceptance. The student facilitated the participants' awareness of unexpected similarities which included two task group members being able to speak to the children, much to the children's delight, in their mother tongue, a language not generally spoken by first language, Afrikaans-speaking South Africans. The attitudes reflected by the participants, as facilitated by the student in the practice example, therefore match the standards set out by the Council on Social Work Education which have shifted from students requiring knowledge about specific populations to a "focus on attitudes and behaviours that reflect appreciation of, respect for, and the ability to practice competently with difference" (Jani, Pierce, Ortiz, & Sowbel in Jani, et al., 2016). The student's reflection refers to the initial introduction of the participants:

I immerse(d) myself in this marvel and natural affinity that was unfolding in front of me, two groups on the extreme end of the spectrum, that have never met before, gelled instantly and at this juncture, nobody cared about social class, race, age or disability they were just united in their diversity and excited about the journey ahead.

Goals achieved include the development of community relations; the acknowledgment of personal power; creating awareness of the similarities of marginalised groups, and an increased tolerance between the different ages, races and cultural backgrounds. Also, the process of transferring skills recognised the often-overlooked aspect of older persons' life experiences and personal strengths as acknowledged by Corey et al. (2010).

As mentioned in the introduction, students' resistance to work with older persons requires attention. Noticeably, not only was the initial resistance of the student addressed, but the student's experience of working with older persons was significantly enriched as is seen in her reflection:

I realised that the residents of the facility just wanted an opportunity and a person that believed in them and their strengths, to make a difference in the lives of other people. Needless to say, it was this project that changed my view about older people and the role they can play in our community when given a chance, and the respect they deserve. Since this project in 2014, I have never looked back in advocating for the rights of older people, changing socio-economic perceptions about older people as well as prevention of their abuse and promotion of their wellbeing.

The importance of the older persons participating in the community-based task group, reflects how being a part of the group, participating and contributing throughout the entire process, holds immense value. The element of participation, essential to the task group work process, truly proved to be the "tool to enhance the quality of life" (Goodrick, 2013:12). However, perhaps the most significant outcome is that group work was at the heart of all the "movement" and transitions in the usually quiet residential care facility.

Conclusion

Societal challenges call on social workers to respond. Internationally, the number of older persons is rapidly on the increase and creative approaches, and implementation of effective service delivery by social workers are required to meet the dynamic needs of this marginalised group. As practice educators, we are tasked to train social workers who can respond to the needs of marginalised groups.

Much has been said about student resistance to working with older persons, and the older persons' lack of enthusiasm to participate in social work interventions. Recognising the significant changes in the profile of older persons offered an opportunity to alter previous approaches to intervention and reflects a valuable response to service delivery. The discussion of an intergenerational skills-transfer programme implemented by a final year social work student in a residential care facility provides a practice example that re-establishes the crucial role of group work with older persons. The older persons, as members of a task group, actively engaged in the planning and implementation of the programme and served as primary drivers throughout the entire process.

Several positive outcomes flowing from the programme are discussed and underscore how group work with older persons can be applied to break down barriers, address resistance and develop relational understanding in communities. The importance of facilitating older persons to continue to offer valuable contributions to their communities reflects the value of addressing relevant needs and formed a significant part of the intervention.

While the use of one practice example is limited in nature, it places focus on the need for further research in this area and highlights the importance of the specific approach to group work with older persons.

Implementing group work, as an integral part of the practice example programme, invites us as social workers to reconsider the powerful role of group work in work with older persons. Considering the approach to group work, as discussed, asks that we recognise the need to rise not only to the challenges in our society but to be creative in the way we address them.

Acknowledgements

This paper is based on the use of group work in the intergenerational skills-transfer programme implemented at the Margaretha Ackerman Residential care facility for Older Persons, SAVF, Pretoria, South Africa.

Sincere thanks are expressed to the Director of Social Services of the SAVF, Ms. Marieta Kemp and social worker and Manager of the Margaretha Ackerman Residential Care Facility, Ms. Hannetjie du Toit, for encouraging and allowing student training in this facility.

A special word of thanks is offered to the fourth-year social work student, Ms. Dithlare Mokhema, for accepting the challenge to address service delivery in work with older persons in a creative manner and for sharing her views in the reflection provided.

References

Allan, L. J. & Johnson, J. A. (2008). Undergraduate Attitudes toward the Elderly: The role of knowledge, contact and aging anxiety, *Educational Gerontology, 35*(1), 1–14. doi:10.1080/03601270802299780

Birkenmaier, J. & Berg-Weger, M. (2017). *The Practice of Generalist Social Work.* (4th ed.). New York and London: Routledge Taylor & Francis Group.

Bloom, D. E., Mitgang, E., & Osher, B. (2016). *Demography of Global Aging. Discussion Paper series.* Retrieved from http://ftp.iza.org/dp10164.pdf

Corey, M. S., Corey, G., & Corey, C. (2010). *Groups: Process and Practice.* (8th ed.). Brooks/Cole: United Kingdom.

Department of Justice and Constitutional Development. (2019). The Older Persons Act, 2006 (13 of 2006) South Africa.

Doel, M. (2006). *Using Groupwork*. London: Routledge Taylor & Francis Group.

DuBois, B. & Miley, K. K. (2014) *Social work: An empowering profession*. (8th ed.). International edition: Pearson.

DuBois, B. & Miley, K. K. (2019). *Social work: An empowering profession*. (9th ed.). International edition: Pearson.

Goodrick, W. F. (2013). Policy implications and challenges of population ageing in South Africa. MA Dissertation. Bloemfontein: University of the Free State.

Jani, J. S., Osteen, P., & Shipe, S. (2016). Cultural Competence and Social Work Education: Moving toward assessment of practice behaviors, *Journal of Social Work Education, 52*(3), 311–324. doi:10.1080/1043779 7.2016.1174634

McAlister, J, Briner, E. L., & Maggi, S. (2019). Intergenerational Programs in Early Childhood Education: An innovative approach that highlights inclusion and engagement with older persons. *Journal of Intergenerational Relationships. 17*(4), 505–522. doi:10.1080/15350770.2019.1618777

Moses, S. (2012). A Just Society for the Elderly: The importance of justice as participation. *Notre Dame Journal of Law, Ethics & Public Policy, Symposium on Aging America. Article 3, 21*(2), 335–362.

Older Persons Act 13 of 2006 (Published in the Government Gazette, (29346) Pretoria: Government Printer).

Panda, A. K. (2005). *Elderly Women in Megapolis: Status and adjustment*. New Delhi: Concept Publishing Company.

Pretorius, E. (2019). Living with Alzheimer's disease in Namibia: The Adult child, the Older Parent and the decision to Institutionalise. MSW Dissertation. Pretoria: University of Pretoria.

Prinsloo, R. (2015). Group intervention with institutionalised older persons. *HTS Teologiese Studies/Theological Studies, 71*(3), 1–7. Retrieved from http://dx.doi.org/10.4102/hts.v71i3.2670

Prinsloo, R. (C. E.). (2019). Cutting and sewing brings Africa to the world: social justice for older people. *Making waves: group work stories of social justice. Social Work with Groups. 43*(3/4), 1–4.

Quinn, A. (2000.) Reluctant Learners: social work students and work with older people. *Research in Post-Compulsory Education, 5*(2), 223–237. doi: 10.1080/13596740000200076

South African National Plan of Development for Older persons. 2005. Policy document. Retrieved from https://www.tafta.org.za/images/ SAPlanofActiononAgeing.pdf

Staples, L. (2004). *Roots to Power: A Manual for Grassroots Organising*. (2nd ed.). USA: Praeger.

Staples, L. (2007). *Social Work Skills for Organising and Leading Task-Oriented Groups*. Focus Homestudy Course. NASW.

United Nations: Department of Economic and Social Affairs, Population Division. (2017a). World Population Ageing 2017. (ST/ESA/SER.A/408)

Walsh, K. Scharf, T., & Keating, N. (2016). Social exclusion of older persons: a scoping review and conceptual framework. *European Journal of Ageing, 14*, 81–98. doi: 10.1007/s10433-016-0398-8

World Health Organisation. (2015). World Report on Ageing and Health. WHO Library Cataloguing-in-Publication Data.

Zastrow, C. H. (2010). *Social Work with Groups: A Comprehensive Workbook.* (7th ed.). United Kingdom: Brooks/Cole.

Community-based care of older people in urban and rural settings in Namibia: Bridging the divide

Janetta Ananias and Leigh Ann Black

Introduction

The aging population is growing rapidly all over the world. According to the World Health Organization, there are currently one billion people worldwide over 60 years of age. By the year 2050, the number of older people is projected to rise to 2 billion, with 80% living in low and middle-income countries (WHO, 2018). Even in sub-Saharan Africa, which has the world's youngest population structure, the number of people over 60 years of age is expected to increase over threefold. The number of older people currently living in the sub-Saharan African region is 46 million, and this number is expected to increase to 165 million by 2050 (WHO, 2017). According to the Population and Housing Census 2011, 7% of Namibians are above the age of 60 years and this number is also projected to increase in years to come (Namibia Statistics Agency, 2013). The increasing number of older people will require a demand in the number of caregivers. The establishment and strengthening of community care systems for older people are of global interest seeing that most care of older people is still informal in both developed and developing countries (United Nations report on aging, 2003).

According to Leiland (2019), many individuals have expressed preferences to remain in the community instead of transitioning to an institutional setting. The costs for institutional care have also forced older people in developed countries to opt for remaining in the communities (De Lange, 2018). To support the desires of older persons to remain in the community, they will need support from caregivers and a network of community health and social services. Caregiving within the community, which is largely done by female family members, is often unpaid and undervalued (Bookman & Kimbrel, 2011). Governments are also saving billions of dollars because of community caregivers (Schulz & Sherwood, 2008). To point out the actual value of caregiving, some scholars already in 2004 estimated that informal care in the United States could cost 257 billion US dollars annually (National Alliance for Caregiving and AARP, 2004).

Informal care systems within community settings can enhance the quality of life of the increasing aging population. Research has shown that taking up a caregiving role can be stressful and burdensome. Signs of chronic stress experienced amongst caregivers are physical and psychological strain over a long period, unpredictable and uncontrollable behaviour, etc. (Schulz, & Sherwood, 2008). Furthermore, many family caregivers reported that they do not have the necessary skill and knowledge to provide sustained care for a person with a chronic condition. As a result, they lack confidence and feel unprepared. Caregivers say that they do not receive guidance from service providers; they do not know how to assume the caregiver role; they are not familiar with the type and amount of care needed, and they do not know how to access and utilize resources (Given, Sherwood, & Given, 2008). A Canadian survey for caregivers of older persons with Alzheimer's disease indicated that caregiving negatively affects the emotional wellbeing of caregivers and led to an increase in financial costs (Bartfay & Bartfay, 2011). Therefore, community-based programmes such as support groups have recently received attention as potentially cost-effective (Bartfay & Bartfay, 2011).

According to Meirung, Visser, and Themistocleus (2017), support groups could offer cost-effective psychosocial interventions to meet the social and emotional needs of caregivers in community settings. Group settings provide opportunities that could improve the quality of life of caregivers and older people. Benefits according to Hsieh, Wang, Yen and Liu (2009) of community-based support groups are that they provide an opportunity for caregivers to reflect and share personal and emotional stressors that are associated with caregiving. Such group exchanges enable caregivers to cope with the stress and emotional burdens associated with caregiving. The involvement of caregivers in support groups offers chances to socialize and therefore reduce the social isolation of caregivers. Although there are many promising approaches, Zarit and Femia (2008) argue that benefits for caregivers are sometimes modest, and some interventions appear to have no or little effect.

From an African perspective, indigenous community-based group work is based on the concept of solidarity, peer support, and mutual aid by group members who come together because of common life experience, common interest, or common need. Examples of such indigenous community-based groups also referred to as self-help groups, can be equated to the ever mushrooming burial societies, income-generating groups like "stokvels," "working groups," youth clubs, and groups addressing various issues emanating from health and social problems. Indigenous community-based groups are a powerful and constructive means for people to help themselves and each other. The basic dignity of each human being is expressed in his or her capacity to be involved in a reciprocal helping exchange. It seems that it is through these indigenous community-based groups that qualities and values embodied in Ubuntu represent an intangible resource that potentially can elevate people to a higher level of social stability and development (Makhubele, 2008). The term Ubuntu is an African concept that is deeply rooted in the community (Letseka, 2012); and is based on the notion that a person depends on others to be a person (Matolino & Kwindingwi, 2013). Likewise, Prinsloo (2015) asserts that groups can be empowering and supportive when group members give and receive feedback to one another. Group work offers members a platform to freely express their feelings and thoughts and learn to realize that they are not alone (Toseland & Rivas, 2012; Zastrow, 2012).

In the Namibian context, community-based groups have been formed for problems such as HIV/AIDS and substance abuse, but this initiative with informal caregivers of older persons will be the first of its kind. Hence, this article presents a community-based initiative for caregivers of older persons in an urban and rural setting.

Background to the group

The need for this community-based group work project was initiated after a needs assessment was carried out that explored the quality of care of older people in urban and rural community settings. The needs assessment was done using in-depth interviews with community leaders, as well as focus group discussions with caregivers and older persons. The needs assessment revealed that family, friends, and neighbours as informal caregivers of older people who live in community settings are experiencing stress and burden. They had no preparation or training on caregiving and were living in social isolation. The exploratory study further found that some older people, especially in rural communities, lived without a family caregiver (Ananias, 2014). Based on the outcome of the needs assessment as well as an extensive literature review, an eight-week programme for caregivers of older persons from urban and rural community settings was proposed. A support group is defined by LaMore (2011) as a place where group members can learn together, deal with feelings of frustration, sadness, or isolation, and receive mutual understanding from each other. Hence, the purpose of this community-based support group was to provide a platform for caregivers of older people from rural and urban community settings to discuss their caregiving experiences and to find better ways to cope with stressful challenging caregiving situations and improving caregiving skills. The group meetings were designed in such a way to encourage caregivers of older persons to talk with others who understood or had gone through similar experiences about the issues, challenges, and decisions they were facing regarding caregiving of an older family member. Group sessions took place weekly over eight weeks, with a follow-up session conducted six weeks after the group came to an end.

The support group members for this community-based programme consisted of informal caregivers who were family members, friends, or neighbours of older persons. Twenty-two female informal caregivers of older people took part in two support groups, with ten caregivers from the urban area in one group and twelve caregivers from the rural area in another group. Caregivers were eligible for the study if they were:

- A child, spouse, sibling, or extended family member as a primary caregiver;
- Assisting an older person with one or more Activities of Daily Living (ADL);
- Willing and available to participate voluntarily for the duration of the programme, and
- Residing in the urban or rural constituency in the Khomas region.

The co-facilitators also formed part of the group composition. The one facilitator was a researcher and group work educator whilst the other facilitator was a novice social worker employed by a State welfare agency responsible for rendering services to older populations. The co-facilitator functioned as a second set of eyes and ears in the group, and paid attention to issues that come up and the reactions of group members. At the end of every group session, a debriefing was done by the group facilitators. The debriefing considered the events in the session, concerns and questions, discussions of group members, and plans for the next group session (Sands & Solomon, 2004). The group sessions for the rural community were held on a Monday afternoon, and the sessions for the urban community were held on Wednesday afternoons. The same theme was covered per week, with each group session lasting between 60 and 90 minutes. The outcome of the group was evaluated using open-ended questions posed to the group members. A comparison between the group members from the rural setting and urban setting as process evaluation was made through a Group Engagement Measure (Macgowan, 2006).

Content of a community-based group work programme for caregivers of older people

The groups aimed to offer support and information to informal caregivers of older people. The opening rituals for every group session consisted of a prayer, a check-in whereby every group member would say something, and an ice-breaker; while the closing rituals entailed a relaxation exercise, verbal evaluation of the group session, and a closing prayer. Incentives for group members were provided in the form of refreshments that were served at the end of every group meeting. The sessions were composed of the following:

Preliminary screening session: An individual interview session was conducted with each prospective group member to ascertain the suitability of membership. A pre-test questionnaire with each group member was also conducted during the recruitment phase to ascertain the level of caregiving that each group participant is involved in. Prospective group members gained an understanding of what the group was all about and confirmed their commitment to participate in the group.

Session One provided an introduction and orientation of the group programme. The co-facilitators welcomed the group members to the first group session and introduced themselves. Member introductions were done using an icebreaker which aimed at reducing anxiety amongst group members who are meeting each other for the first time and to create a relaxed atmosphere in the group. Group participants were requested to arrange themselves in a line that represents the length of time they have been a caregiver to the older care recipient, from the shortest time of caregiving to the longest time. To figure out who has spent time as a caregiver and where they should be in the line, group participants were instructed to interact with one another. Another round of member introductions was done, and members were instructed to form subgroups according to their relationship with the older care recipient (for example spouse, adult child, sibling, and more), and to introduce themselves in the subgroup with their name and their relationship with the older care recipient. The members were asked to form a new subgroup, and again introduce themselves, until each group member contacted several group members.

Before the group facilitators stated the purpose of the group, the members were requested to express their expectations for joining the group. The group members in both urban and rural settings had some difficulty in formulating expectations since they tend to concentrate more on their caregiver role in terms of the problems care recipients experience instead of their own needs, thus the group facilitators gently steered members to start to think about their expectations as participants of the support group. The establishment of a relationship with co-facilitators of the group and with fellow group members was accomplished in both groups in the urban and rural setting while contracting towards the group rules and completion of the programme took place verbally due to the lower literacy levels of some of the group members. Group members from both urban and rural settings were very enthusiastic about the group and were looking forward to the upcoming group meetings.

Session Two provided an overview of the normal process of aging. An experiential exercise was introduced as an icebreaker to illustrate the difficulties older people experience with mobility, vision, and senses because of the normal processes of aging. The experiential exercise enabled group members to share their thoughts and concerns as they were thinking about their aging. The simulation exercises and group discussions helped both the urban and rural groups understand the biological, psychological, and social processes of aging and to show more sensitivity towards the older care recipient. They also understood and shared how these aging processes related to their caregiving experiences.

Many myths or misconceptions exist around aging in general, therefore group members were presented with true/false statements on aging. Stereotypes that caregivers had around aging were thereafter corrected. Co-facilitators provided a lecture on the normal processes of aging with handouts provided to each caregiver at the end of the group meeting. Group members from both the urban and rural groups had a positive experience of the group meeting. One group member in the rural setting disclosed how she had acted insensitively towards her care recipient out of a lack of knowledge about the normal processes of aging and resolved to change her attitude as a caregiver.

Session Three focused on handling difficult caregiving situations. Group participants were requested to form pairs and to identify the challenging behaviours they encounter because of caregiving and the current ways how they are dealing with these problem situations. The pairs then reported back to the group. In the discussions, caregivers listed difficult caregiving situations they experienced and eventually solutions were sought for these identified problems. Common difficult caregiving situations listed by both the urban and rural group included, amongst others, older people's refusal to bathe; dependence of older people on one caregiver only; swearing and insults by some older people towards the caregiver; mental illness behaviours displayed by some older people; sleep deprivation of caregivers due to demand to constantly monitor older people's behaviour, and the difficulty for caregivers to find any help.

Specific difficulties reported by the group of rural caregivers included challenges in caring for bedridden older care recipients; gender sensitivity in terms of a male caregiver providing care to a female care recipient; age sensitivity about the care recipient-caregiver dyad; difficulty on the part of the caregiver to exercise patience; challenges in communicating with an older person with a hearing problem; dealing with overly-demanding older care recipients; the habitual use of snuff, pipe or smoking by some older people; and the lack of transport for older people with mobility problems.

Through mutual aid, group members could make suggestions to one another for difficulties faced because of caregiving. Some suggestions shared among group members were a delegation of responsibilities amongst family members, doing proper planning, accepting situations that cannot be changed, and praying. Group members from the urban group further suggested that bathing of the older male care recipients can be done by a male family or community member or an older person's peer acceptable to the older care recipient as a solution. The importance of exercising patience was identified by the rural group as an important aspect to consider for caregivers.

Session Four focused on caregiver stress. After the topic caregiver stress was introduced and defined, group members formed smaller groups to share their stressors related to caregiving, which was subsequently reported to the bigger group. Group members from the rural group shared several stressors which were amongst others, being called frequently by the care recipient; the lack of finances or income; the irritable behaviour displayed by some older care recipients, especially when they do not have tobacco or snuff; lack of appreciation by some older care recipients; the death of loved ones; and substance abuse by some care recipients. Concerning substance abuse, one group member disclosed multiple caregiver stressors caused by the care recipient's substance abuse problem, refusal to bath himself, and the extreme condition of self-neglect. The caregiver has not received any help despite reporting the problem to the relevant authorities. Emotional support was granted to the aggrieved caregiver who felt embarrassed and helpless for the neglectful situation of the care recipient, and a referral was made for individual medical and social interventions.

Signs and symptoms of caregiver stress were displayed on a flipchart by co-facilitators, and all group members from the urban and rural settings agreed that caregiver stress affects their health and wellbeing. Four ways to deal with stress were discussed by the group members as ways to deal with stress, namely, asking for help, acceptance, taking care of one's health, and finding some time off from caregiving. One group member from the urban area reported how delegating caregiving tasks amongst family members had lessened her caregiver burden. In response to keeping a healthy lifestyle, several group members from the urban group disclosed their weaknesses about indulging in sweet foodstuffs. Group members encouraged each other to start eating healthy food as a way of dealing with stress. A stress-relieving exercise in the form of a massage was enjoyed by all the group members and became a part of the group rituals.

Session Five emphasized the importance of self-care of the caregiver. An imagination exercise was used to introduce the topic of self-care, as group members had to imagine facing a dilemma, whereby they had to choose between their own needs or the needs of the care recipient. As part of the exercise, most group members in both the urban and rural setting opted to respond to the needs of the older care recipient instead of their own. After some time debating, group members realized the detrimental consequences on both the caregiver and the care-recipient, if the needs of caregivers are ignored. Group members explored the reasons why caregivers were not keen to care for themselves, which were ascribed by group members to socialisation and culture. Group members discussed how the absence of self-care could lead to poor interpersonal relationships, to potential verbal abuse towards the older care recipients, and the poor health of caregivers. Group members of the rural group assisted one group member who was faced with a dilemma between either to receive medical help and to leave the older care recipient unattended for a short while or to ignore her health and continue caregiving responsibilities.

To strengthen the importance of self-care, the rights of caregivers were placed on a flipchart and discussed in the group. Group members from both the urban and rural groups found the information on the rights of caregivers informative and insightful. Group members shared caregiving experiences where these rights were violated, and the support group offered an environment where group members could vent their emotions. Self-care strategies grouped under the physical, social, emotional, and spiritual dimensions were placed on the flipchart. After these self-care strategies were explained, group members assisted one another to develop a balanced self-care plan. As part of the homework assignment, group members continued to work on an individualized self-care plan.

Session Six focused on elder abuse and neglect. The topic of "elder abuse" was introduced with a brief history of World Elder Abuse Awareness Day celebrated on 15 June. Posters on World Elder Abuse Awareness Day (WEAAD) and the United Nations Principles for Older Persons, 1991 were displayed on the walls. After a brief explanation of the rights of older persons, group members were asked to draw a picture of their emotions whenever they hear about elder abuse. Group members managed to draw images about abuse and shared their pictures with the group. Based on the pictures, group members could point out the various forms of elder abuse, such as financial abuse, emotional abuse, sexual abuse, partner violence, and neglect. Group members from the rural area pointed out that poor emergency transport services lead to the neglect of older persons to access health care.

The perceptions of group members on restraint, as a form of elder abuse, gave rise to some discussion on an incident in the rural setting where restraint did occur. The discussion helped group members realize that restraint is also a violation of the right of older persons. In community settings where older persons live in extended family settings, abuse of the older person may be perpetrated by another family member and not by the primary caregiver per se. Group members from the rural setting have limited access to government agencies where elder abuse can be reported while the group members from the urban setting were able to mention government, private, and faith-based agencies that could assist with complaints of elder abuse.

Session Seven emphasized grief and loss that caregivers may experience. The topic of grief and loss was introduced by the co-facilitators, with the concepts "grief" and "loss" defined. Further differentiation was made between a "tangible" loss and "psychological" loss. Group members were requested to discuss the psychological losses they had experienced, and their feelings associated with these losses. Group members from the rural setting were resistant and uncomfortable talking about their losses since long silences were observed. In the urban setting, group members rather revealed some tangible losses instead of psychological losses. However, two members from the urban area, who had expressed emotional reactions about psychological losses in previous group sessions, received an opportunity to share their emotions. Group members were not as emotional as expected by the co-facilitators but instead shared how their faith in God helped them get through those difficult times of grief and loss. The phases of loss, according to Kübler-Ross (1969), were displayed on a flipchart. Group members from the urban area were more engaged in recognizing feelings of guilt, denial, and acceptance they have experienced than the rural group. The four ways to cope with grief listed on the flipchart were discussed, namely, self-care, awareness, and expression of emotions, as well as talking to a professional or religious leader, and finally developing a support network. Group members could identify the various people they regarded as their support network for issues on grief and loss but also caregiving in general.

Session Eight was done to terminate the groups. The termination session was attended by some officials from the State welfare agency and representatives from the church as special guests. As group members reviewed their expectations set at the beginning of the group, both members from the urban and rural groups expressed satisfaction that their expectations were met. To consolidate their learning, group members highlighted the lessons learned throughout the group process. The certificates of attendance were awarded to each group member, who felt happy and proud to receive them. Since members expressed their desire for the continuation of the support group amongst the caregivers, a coordinator who will be responsible to collaborate with the social worker regarding future support group activities was elected and introduced. Sustainability of community initiatives is an important aspect of continuity. Therefore, the social worker from the State welfare agency who co-facilitated the group will continue to hold monthly meetings with the members of the support group. Furthermore, ideas to replicate this community initiative to other constituencies and regions in Namibia were expressed.

The last Follow-up session was done six weeks after the groups were terminated. The follow-up session aimed to once again review the lessons learned and applied since the group's termination, to discuss the way forward. All the objectives of the follow-up session were met. The respondents from both urban and rural areas still clearly recalled lessons learned that they could apply since the group has ended on caregiver stress and the importance of self-care.

The respondents from the rural area were still concerned about the number of older people without any caregiver, as well as hospitalized older people who are neglected, while the respondents from the urban group were concerned about the substance abuse of older people, some bedridden older people who need help, as well as the poor care and control of older persons from the old age home. The group members mentioned that these concerns be attended to as part of the way forward. The groups ended after everybody offered final feedback on the value of the programme. Once again, caregivers expressed their appreciation for the programme. The social worker then announced the days when the monthly meetings would be held.

Conclusion

This paper attempted to draw some light on a community-based social work intervention with informal caregivers of older people in an urban and rural setting. It appears that the programme objectives have been achieved as the group participants indeed obtained more information about caregiving, and group members were able to support one another. From the evaluations done at the termination and follow up sessions, members could highlight that lessons around self- care and handling of difficult caregiving situations stood out for them. Organizing respite care in a community-based setting is feasible, as a caregiver in an extended family set up could rearrange duties around caregiving amongst family members. In addition to offering education and support, community-based caregivers indicated in the evaluations that they also require basic resources such as soap, ointment, bandages bed linen, and others. Rural communities highlighted challenges with transporting older persons in need of medical attention.

The Group Engagement Measure (Macgowan, 2006) was used to evaluate how engaged group members were to the intervention, and to compare engagements between rural and urban groups. The group engagement measure indicated that the urban group was more engaged than the rural group in all the domains. Caregivers from rural communities are from a closer community and may be related to one another, which is not the case in urban communities. Therefore, caregivers from the rural group may assume that it is not necessary to share their struggles that are already known in the community in a support group and they also had concerns around privacy. Despite groups from rural communities being less engaged, their eagerness to learn and attend was observed in their punctuality and attendance of the group session. Implications for practitioners of future groups are that as much as we invest in urban communities, there is a need to also make services equally available for communities in rural areas. Indeed, the need for community interventions is much higher in rural areas than in urban areas.

This community-based intervention can be expanded to other constituencies and regions in Namibia. Indeed, African communities and the rest of the world can also take lessons from this community-based intervention. If we need to respond to the complex needs of caregivers and the older care recipients, a social development approach needs to be adopted, and more role-players in addition to social workers need to come on board. Community-based caregivers need resources to take care of the older care recipient, but some may not have any other income. Therefore, income-generating activities and skills building of caregivers need to be considered.

References

Ananias, J. A. (2014). An evaluation of social work support groups with informal caregivers to prevent elder abuse and neglect: A Namibian perspective. Ph.D. Thesis. North-West University: Potchefstroom Campus.

Bartfay, E. & Bartfay, W. J. (2011). Quality-of-Life outcomes among Alzheimer's Disease family caregivers following community-based intervention. *Western Journal of Nursing, 35*(1), 98–116.

De Lange, F. (2018). Is home the best place to be old? The changing geography of responsibilities in the care for elderly. *Stellenbosch Theological Journal, 4*(1), 133–151.

Given, B., Sherwood, P. R., & Given, C. W. (2008). What knowledge and skills do caregivers need? *Journal of Social Work Education, 44*(3), 115–123, doi:10.5175/JSWE.2008.773247703

Hsieh, H. F., Wang, J. J., Yen, M., & Liu, T. T. (2009). Educational support group in changing caregiver's psychological elder abuse behavior towards caring for institutionalized elders. *Advances in health science education, 14*, 377–386.

Kübler-Ross, E. (1969). *On death and dying.* London: Tavistock.

LaMore, K. W. (2011). Use of Alzheimer family support group by community residing caregivers. *Group Work, 21*(2), 84–98, doi:10.1921/095182411X613315

Leiland, N. E. (2019). Book Review: Home- and community-based services for older adults aging in context. *Journal of Applied Gerontology, 38*(10), 1506–1508.

Letseka, M. (2012). In defense of Ubuntu. *Studies in Philosophy and Education, 31*, 47–60. https://doi.org/10.1007/s11217-011-9267-2

Macgowan, M. J. 2006. The group engagement measure: A review of its conceptual and empirical properties. *Journal of groups in addiction and recovery, 1*(2):33– 52

Makhubele, J. (2008). The impact of indigenous community-based groups towards social development. *Indilinga African Journal of Indigenous Knowledge Systems, 7*(1), 37–46.

Matolino, B. & Kwindingwi, W. (2013). The end of Ubuntu, *South African Journal of Philosophy, 32*(2), 197–205, doi:10.1080/02580136.2013.817637

Meirung, L., Visser, M., & Themistocleus, N. (2017). A student-facilitated community-based support group initiative for Mental Health Care users in a Primary Health Care setting, *Health SA Gesondheid, 22*(1), 307–315.

National Statistics Agency (NSA), (2013). Namibia Population and Housing

Census.

Prinsloo, R. (2015). Group intervention with institutionalised older persons, *HTS Teologiese Studies/Theological Studies*, *71*(3), 1–7, http://dx.doi.org/10.4102/ hts.v71i3.2670

Sands, R. G. & Solomon, P. (2004). Developing educational groups in Social Work Practice, *Social Work with Groups*, *26*(2), 5–21.

Schulz, R. & Sherwood, P. R. (2008). Physical and mental health effects of family caregiving, *Journal of Social Work Education*, *44*(3), 105–113, doi:10.5175/JSWE.2008.773247702

United Nations General Assembly, (1991). United Nations Principles for Older Persons. Adopted by General Assembly Resolution 46/91 of 16 December 1991.

World Health Organization (WHO), (2017). Integrated care for older people. Guidelines on community-level interventions to manage declines in intrinsic capacity. Geneva: Switzerland.

World Health Organization (WHO), (2018). The Global Network for Age-friendly Cities and Communities Looking back over the last decade, looking forward to the next, Geneva: Switzerland.

Zarit, S. & Femia, E. (2008). Behavioral and psychosocial interventions for family caregivers, *Journal of Social Work Education*, *44*(3), 49–57, doi:10.5175/JSWE.2008.773247711

Perceptions of a group work batterer intervention program for intimate partner violence perpetrators

Michael J. Lyman, Cheyenne K. Port, Michelle M. Cousins, Emily E. Stottlemyer, Monica R. DeCarlo, Paige A. Bankhead-Lewis and Adolfo Alvarez

Introduction

Intimate Partner Violence was recently linked to issues of social justice in a brief from the NASW (National Association of Social Workers) (2018) and has been described as:

> A serious and persistent life-threatening criminal and public health problem affecting millions of people each year across the United States. IPV is prevalent in every socioeconomic group, regardless of race or ethnicity. Because of the pervasiveness of IPV, especially with women as the primary victim, it is not only a criminal justice and public health crisis but also has enormous child welfare implications. Moreover, the emotional toll that the trauma of physical, sexual, and psychological abuse takes on its survivors can last for a lifetime (p. 1).

The problem of intimate partner violence is addressed through a variety of interventions for both victims and perpetrators, however, a recent review of evidence-based interventions for the perpetrators of such violence suggested that after traditional arrest and criminal proceedings, the standard approach is group treatment intervention (Stover, Meadows & Kaufman, 2009). Group interventions have been identified as the tool of choice to target change in batterers' perceptions of accountability. Facilitators can create group norms and use peer dynamics to focus on the problematic attitudes and behaviors of new members. The dynamics of a group-based intervention in these programs are also effective in challenging and confronting the perpetrator, as well as providing numerous psychoeducational opportunities (Aguirre, Lehmann, & Patton, 2011).

The project discussed in this paper is a multi-faceted exploration of the AMEND program, which is a group-based batterer intervention program based on the Duluth model (Pence & Paymar, 1993). The two prongs of the project involved 1) a document analysis focusing on recidivism among former participants of the AMEND program, and 2) a report on the analysis of qualitative interviews conducted with six previous AMEND program participants.

Literature Review

Intimate partner violence

According to the Centers for Disease Control, Intimate Partner Violence (IPV) is described as physical, sexual, or psychological harm by a current or former partner or spouse and can include physical violence, sexual violence, and psychological and emotional violence (Herman, Rotunda, Williamson, & Vodanovich, 2014; Breiding, Basile, Smith, Black, & Mahendra, 2015). Interpersonal Violence (IPV) can be found across all demographics (Ventura, Lambert, White, & Skinner, 2007). One in five couples will experience at least one IPV episode this year (Scott & Easton, 2010) and one in six women will be a victim of attempted or successful rape during her lifetime (Powell & Smith, 2011). A majority of IPV that is committed (64%) is a simple assault (Truman & Morgan, 2014), however sexual assault or forced sex occurs in 40-45 percent of battering relationships' lifetime (Powell & Smith, 2011). Overall, 45% of reported incidents of IPV resulted in injury to the victim (Truman & Morgan, 2014). In most cases of IPV, the perpetrator is a former or current boyfriend (39%) or spouse (25%) (Truman & Morgan, 2014). Unfortunately, only about 55% of IPV acts are reported to the police (Truman & Morgan, 2014). This under-reporting of domestic violence is often the result of shame, embarrassment, self-blame, fear of further injury, exposure, retaliation, and fear of reliving the violence through a trial (Powell & Smith, 2011). There is much to be considered when dealing with a problem like intimate partner violence, and one somewhat under-appreciated aspect of this phenomenon is the treatment opportunities for the perpetrators.

Batterer intervention programs

Many domestic violence perpetrators are court-mandated to attend anger management-focused programs, which emphasize individual deficits and the management of negative emotions (Day, Chung, O'Leary & Carson, 2009). An alternative to anger management programs is batterer intervention programs which include open-ended, psycho-educational, and gender-specific groups (Price & Rosenbaum, 2009; Tollefson, Webb, Shumway, Block, & Nakamura, 2009). In many criminal courts dealing with family violence, batterer intervention programs (BIP) have become an alternative punishment for offenders of IPV or domestic violence. The majority, about 90–95%, of BIP participants are court-ordered into these interventions (Solinas-Saunders & Thaller, 2015). Some participants may also be referred through Child Protective Services (Solinas-Saunders & Thaller, 2015). Many of the batterer intervention programs that these perpetrators are referred to are based on the Duluth model of batterer intervention (Aguirre, Lehmann, & Patton, 2011; Pence & Paymar, 1993), which is one of the most recognized treatment approaches with the IPV perpetrator population.

The Duluth Model which was originally proposed by Pence and Paymar (1993) and is based on the theory that violence is used to control the victim's behavior. Interventions are intended to take place in collaboration with community resources which use their institutional influence to diminish the power of the perpetrator over their victim[s]. The group dynamics and educational interventions that occur in a Duluth Model program are designed to help batterers explore the intent and source of their violent behaviors as well as the possibility of changing the types and quality of relationships they have with women (Pence & Paymar, 1993). The model itself is feminist-informed and sees violence in intimate relationships resulting from cultural and patriarchal beliefs about men's power and control over women. The Duluth model also challenges the common myth that violence is a result of psychological or behavior problems in the perpetrator, instead, the model encourages perpetrator accountability and an eventual break down of denial and rationalization/justification. Because of these underlying assumptions of the Duluth model, practitioners of the model do not see traditional batterer treatments focused on anger management as an effective response to the problem of intimate partner violence (Aguirre, Lehmann, & Patton, 2011).

Because of the Duluth Model's alternative view of batterer intervention, it has proven successful in many instances in reducing recidivism among perpetrators of intimate partner violence. Most research assessing recidivism for batterer intervention program completers versus non-completers shows that those who do not complete the BIP generally have higher rates of recidivism than those who complete the program (Herman, et al., 2014). However, a recent meta-analysis of the effectiveness of batterer intervention programs concluded that the results are inconclusive when it comes to the positive influence of such programs (Arias, Arce & Vilariño, 2013). Similar conclusions from another meta-analysis were reported by Stover, et al. (2009), though their characterization is that there is a lack of evidence of effectiveness for such programs when compared to arrest alone. A recent large-scale evaluation found equally low performance in recidivism reduction in these batterer intervention programs that follow the Duluth model – the same model followed in the AMEND program (Herman, et al., 2014). However, other evaluations of these types of programs have shown a reduction in recidivism rates from 25% to a mere 5% among perpetrators (Arias, et al., 2013). Due to the Duluth model's apparent success, several programs based on the model have been established to deal with the problem of intimate partner violence.

The AMEND program

The AMEND program (AMEND, n.d.) is based on the Duluth Model (Aguirre, Lehmann, & Patton, 2011; Pence & Paymar, 1993) and seeks to treat perpetrators of interpersonal violence with an emphasis on personal responsibility and recognizing and controlling abusive behavior. Generally, programs based on the Duluth model cannot exist in a community where services are not provided for domestic violence victims. Fortunately, in Cumberland and Perry Counties in central Pennsylvania, such services are available and the AMEND program has been functioning in its present form for over seven years. AMEND is a group-based program offered in 28 sessions through the Domestic Violence Services of the local counties. This program is available for men who have committed intimate partner violence (AMEND, n.d.). The participants are court-mandated or attend voluntarily (AMEND, n.d.). AMEND uses the education curriculum from the Duluth Abuse Intervention Project entitled "Power and Control: Tactics of Men Who Batter" (AMEND, n.d.).

In this Duluth curriculum or "Duluth Model" there are four guiding principles: 1) Removing the blame for the abuse from the victim and placing accountability on the offender/perpetrator; 2) Prioritizing the voices and perspectives of women who experience battering in the creating of related policies and procedures; 3) Believing that battering is a pattern of actions intended to control and dominate an intimate partner; and 4) Challenging participants to think critically about their assaultive choices (AMEND, n.d.). These feminism-inspired principles help perpetrators to challenge the predominant patriarchal views of power and control in intimate relationships and take accountability for their violent behaviors.

The core principles of the AMEND (n.d.) program and other batterer intervention programs based on the Duluth model are safety, accountability, and collaboration/coordination. The most important goal in a BIP like AMEND is to ensure that the safety of the victim can be achieved, thus safety is the first principle of the AMEND program and engagement with the victim – even in a treatment setting – is not recommended. This means that programs like AMEND are not co-educational, meaning that they are not intended to be coupled with the treatment of other potentially co-occurring problems. The focus is on the violent behaviors of the perpetrator. This means that proponents of programs like AMEND do not accept that substance abuse treatment, mental illness intervention, anger management, or couples counseling are appropriate or safe substitutions for intervening in a relationship where battering is taking place. Couple's counseling is never recommended by AMEND staff, because the accountability of the perpetrator for his behaviors is the primary focus, thus completion of the BIP is the primary focus.

The principle of accountability is expressed in the program's assurance that violent behavior is seen as a choice, not an impulsive act, an intentional act, and not a result of poor anger management (AMEND, n.d.). Instead, participants are taught that they are responsible for the actions in every situation. In other words, according to the Duluth model and the AMEND program, domestic or intimate partner violence is not a relationship problem, but a problem of violent behaviors/choices in an abusive individual.

Collaboration and coordination in the AMEND (n.d.) program are evident as the program staff work with affiliated domestic violence service entities, (e.g. law enforcement, the judiciary, and others) to establish relationships and a general community attitude that does not condone or accept violent behaviors. Specifically, AMEND staff hopes to advocate for a change in perspective where intimate violence is seen as an issue of violent choices and not problematic anger.

The AMEND program starts with an initial assessment to determine the participant's appropriateness for the program. What follows is 28 sessions including 26 weekly interactive structured group sessions and two individual sessions that take place at weeks 13 and 26. The group sessions are always facilitated by both female and male facilitators. At a basic level, the components of the AMEND program are structured around education, values examination, and behavioral challenge, to help men put their behavior in the larger social context of male socialization and teach egalitarian strategies for decision making, communication, and conflict resolution (AMEND, n.d.). The group context assists in achieving the goals of safety and accountability that the AMEND program outlines for its participants, through familiar group processes such as mutual aid, peer-based challenges of dysfunctional thinking, and generally positive support for change (Toseland & Rivas, 2012). Specific curricular content for the group sessions helps to embed psychoeducational interventions into these group processes.

Specifically, the focus of the AMEND program curriculum is the Equality and Power and Control Wheels (AMEND, n.d.), which focuses on helping participants understand their patriarchal and controlling thinking about their victims. The wheels, presented in eight basic themes, are explored over the 26 weeks of the program. The positive and nonviolent behaviors taught in the group sessions are meant to replace the controlling and abusive behaviors the program hopes to help end (AMEND, n.d.). These positive behaviors are encouraged through peer interactions within the group and positive reinforcement from program facilitators.

Methodology: Document analysis

The document analysis portion of this assessment involved collecting public criminal record data of IPV perpetrators to determine the potential impact of AMEND program participation on recidivism rates.

Setting and context

Initially, the director of the AMEND program suggested that the researchers collect data on recidivism measures for those mandated to anger management and compare them to the men who participated in the AMEND program. As the data collection portion of this project commenced the researchers quickly discovered that, to their credit, judges were not referring intimate partner violence perpetrators to anger management programs in any great numbers. Thus, the aim of the project was altered somewhat. Researchers decided that a simple qualitative comparison of the AMEND program participants and non-participants who were also domestic violence perpetrators would meet the needs of the AMEND program staff in the absence of an adequate anger management comparison group. Thus, the resulting new purpose for this portion of the assessment was to determine, using simple document analysis, if the group dynamics of batterer intervention programs, such as AMEND, affect intimate partner violence perpetrators' chance of reoffending.

Data collection

The recidivism data (number of arrests and bail amount) for both the AMEND and anger management participants are a matter of public record and were collected through the assistance of the AMEND program itself, the Cumberland County District Attorney's office, and the Office of Victims Services in Cumberland County, Pennsylvania. The available data included the following: 1) records from the AMEND program, including participants' age, ethnicity, residence, referral agency, attendance dates, and completion dates; 2) records from the

District Attorney's office on whether the participants re-offended after the AMEND program, and 3) records from the Cumberland County Victim Services on all intimate partner violence perpetrators for the year of 2015. These records provided basic demographic data and a series of indicators that the researchers used to operationally define recidivism.

Once the researchers had obtained appropriate approval from the university Institutional Review Board, the AMEND program provided the participation data from the 2015 calendar year for their program to the researchers. The names on these AMEND records were then compared to the records for the same period from both the District Attorney's office and the Victim Services offices to assess whether the non-AMEND participants and the AMEND graduates re-offended and to what extent. This comparison of these two groups was thus a simple qualitative document analysis of the two groups to identify relevant trends or themes that will inform future programming decisions and advocacy efforts at the AMEND program.

One of the difficulties in this process of data collection from extant criminal files was the fact that in the Commonwealth of Pennsylvania there are no crimes specifically characterized as "intimate partner violence" or "domestic violence." Thus, the data collection process became quite complex as the researchers had to look at each file and determine if the victim of the crime was an intimate partner. For example, if the researchers found a file where the simple assault was the crime, they then had to read the actual case file and description of the incident to determine if the victim of the assault was a domestic partner or spouse.

Operational definition of recidivism

The researchers were able to collect data describing the number of perpetrators arrested, the total number of arrests (because perpetrators could be arrested more than once), the number of incarcerations, the number of days incarcerated, the cost of incarceration, and total bail amount assessed to the re-offending perpetrators. This collection of variables became the operational definition of recidivism for this qualitative document analysis.

Methodology: Participant interviews

The interview portion of this project involved interviews with past AMEND program participants who completed telephone interviews with members of the research team.

Sample

The sample of this study consisted of six men, at least the age of 18, who completed the AMEND program in the recent past. A total of ten potential participants were identified by the AMEND program facilitators and six responded to the request to conduct an interview.

Protection of research participants

The research procedures were approved by the Shippensburg University Committee on Research with Human Subjects before conducting any data collection. Before conducting the interviews, the researchers read and reviewed the informed consent with all participants. The informed consent included information on the purpose of the research study, the participant's rights, and the participant's consent to participate in the phone interview. All participants acknowledged that they were at least 18 years old and understood their rights and voluntary participation in the study before beginning the interview.

The researchers did not collect the names of any interviewees and each interviewee was randomly assigned a number to track and organize the interviews. Caution was also exercised to remove any identifying information such as participants' names, names of intimate partners or family members, and participants' phone numbers during the transcription process. Names of intimate partners were also not included in the data set and the participants' phone numbers were shredded following the interviews to ensure confidentiality.

Data collection

Staff from the AMEND program identified participants who had completed the program during the recent past. Phone numbers were also provided by agency staff. The telephone interviews took place over approximately four weeks. An interview schedule was developed with open and closed-ended questions designed to guide the researchers during the interview. The telephone interviews ranged from approximately 5 minutes to 20 minutes in length, depending on the responses and cooperation of the participant.

Data analysis

Telephone interviews were transcribed by the research team and written up in Microsoft Word. The transcribed interviews were then imported to NVivo 10 for analysis. Several themes/nodes were identified throughout the analysis including the following: domestic violence crimes, Protection from Abuse violation, police calls, intimate relationships, social media/harassment, program values, abusive behaviors, learned skills, pornography, program satisfaction, program dissatisfaction, program recommendations, and future contact. The researchers used sub-nodes and other features of the NVivo software to further analyze the results.

Findings: Document analysis

Absence of referrals to anger management programs

One of the unexpected findings from this research process was the surprising but pleasant discovery that judges are not referring perpetrators of domestic violence to anger management programs. No referrals to anger management programs were identified in the records search of the participants in this part of the project. While this discovery forced a change in the focus of this project it was a promising finding from the perspective of the staff at the AMEND program. The data collection process confirmed that judges are not referring violators of protective orders to anger management programs.

Demographics of the comparison groups

Table 1 below provides a demographic comparison of the two groups assessed in this project. As expected, only a small number of men can participate and complete the AMEND program in any given year. In 2015, 15 men completed the full 26-week program and successfully graduated. There were more men in 2015 in Cumberland County who were domestic violence perpetrators who were not referred to the AMEND program. Despite the difference in numbers, with the limited demographic data available from the records, the two groups are comparable in terms of the average age, however, there are some slight variations in the racial demographics of the two groups.

Table 1

Demographics of the Comparison Groups

Completed the AMEND Program		No Program	
Participants in the group	15	Participants in the group	44
Average age	34.87	Average age	36.53
Race/Ethnicity		Race/Ethnicity	
Caucasian	10 (67%)	Caucasian	41 (93%)
African American	0	African American	2 (5%)
Asian	2 (13%)	Asian	0
Biracial	1 (7%)	Biracial	0
Other/ Undocumented	2 (13%)	Other/ Undocumented	1 (2%)

Recidivism outcomes

The following two tables summarize the recidivism outcomes for the two groups of men studied in this project. The differences across these variables for the two groups should be readily apparent. Of note is the financial impact of the recidivism as represented by the difference in costs associated with days incarcerated and total bail amounts.

Table 2

Criminal data for the comparison groups

Completed the AMEND Program		No Program	
%Arrested	13.33%	%Arrested	15.90%
Number arrested	2	Number arrested	7
Number of arrests	2	Number of arrests	8
Number incarcerated	1	Number incarcerated	7
Days incarcerated	1	Days incarcerated	131
Cost for incarceration	$117.06	Cost for incarceration	$15,334.90
Total bail amount	$1,000.00	Total bail amount	$155,000.00

Table 3 shows a cumulative list of all the charges that members of the two groups faced in the months after their arrest for a domestic violence incident. It is presented here simply as a means of providing a qualitative comparison of the types of crimes each group was charged with. Crimes were only listed once, thus the list simply reflects the variety of crimes committed by members of each group, not the numbers of crime committed. Nearly all the crimes listed here were specifically or related to domestic violence-related behaviors.

Table 3

Charges for the Comparison Groups

Completed the AMEND Program	No Program
Simple assault Harassment subject to other physical contacts	Simple assault Disorderly conduct Harassment Involuntary deviate sexual intercourse – person unconscious Sexual assault Driving under the influence Possession of firearm prohibited Aggravated assault Criminal mischief Felony aggravated assault Endangering the welfare of children Disorderly conduct, engage in fighting

Findings: Participant Interviews

Criminal acts following the AMEND program

Of the six interview participants, none reported committing crimes relating to intimate partner violence since the completion of the AMEND program. Also, all of the participants reported that they had not been subject to a Protection from Abuse order since the completion of the AMEND program. In response to a question regarding police calls, every participant in the sample reported that no police calls were made relating to domestic violence situations. Additionally, 100% of the sample reported that they have not harassed anyone, including using social media, since completing the AMEND program.

Family and relationships

Since the completion of the AMEND program, only one of the six interview participants was in a new relationship, four participants reported being in the same relationship, and one participant was neither with the same partner nor in a new relationship. Questioning relating to pornography yielded more mixed results. Three of the participants reported that they watched pornography before and after completing the AMEND program. The other half of the sample reported that they did not watch pornography before or after completing the AMEND program.

Maintenance of program goals

All the interview participants agreed with the statement that their behaviors have been consistent with the AMEND program values since leaving the program. When asked to explain, participants mentioned that they were continuing to treat women with respect, valuing fairness with their partner, acknowledging when to leave a situation when triggered, and some referenced a specific part of the curriculum- the equality wheel- as a necessary part of their maintenance. One participant stated, "The program opened my eyes to mental and verbal abuse as well, and what is abuse. I approach my partner in a better manner. It helped me personally, so it changed how I approach my partner, my family, even my boss at work."

Participants also identified the following specific areas of growth during their interview: awareness, listening, negotiating, peer influences, and utilizing therapy or counseling. One participant stated that the following was an important factor in his progress: "realizing that I can't control what others believe or think or say. I am only in control of myself and my actions." Half of the sample reported learning to recognize triggers and behaviors that may cause them to become angry or aggressive. Another participant stated, "I try not to identify with anyone abusive, male or female. I exit myself from any bad situation." One of the six participants indicated that he sought out counseling services and continues to participate three times per week in therapy. Two of the participants reported that they use the skills learned in the AMEND program daily, while one participant uses them weekly or biweekly and the other participant rarely uses the learned skills from the AMEND program.

Satisfaction with the AMEND program and recommendations

Participants were particularly open to discussing the AMEND program itself and their recommendations for the program. Two participants identified the three facilitators as the most positive part of the AMEND program. Five participants credited the group dynamics as their favorite part of the program. The same number, but different participants, stated the ability to be self-aware was the strongest part of the program. Three participants agreed that the educational tools they received from the program were not only helpful during the program, but were helpful after completing the program, as well. These participants continue to use the tools to maintain healthy and safe intimate relationships. All participants agreed that peer learning was a major factor in their successful completion of the program. All participants agreed that being able to have someone that they could relate to and not feel alone was a major component of what made the program enjoyable and successful. The group context thus contributed to their positive experiences (Toseland & Rivas, 2012).

When discussing program dissatisfaction, one participant had a criticism of the course relating to the course material. Specifically, this participant stated that "the male administrator's strong personality in the beginning of the program," and length of the program – "I didn't like how long it was but I know the time it takes is needed" – were identified as problematic. Accountability and the group dynamics were mentioned as a dislike as an uncomfortable asset, but something that other participants also enjoyed about the program. Along with this group dynamic, one participant stated that they did not get along well with fellow group members.

Recommendations for the AMEND program were also gathered from the interview participants. Some participants enjoyed the program so much, they had no recommendations for improvement. Two participants requested more efficient collaboration stating, "I would change that the fee goes to court costs." This comment related to the multiple disciplinary teams working together to help the male batterers get into the group faster to complete their mandate in a timelier manner. One participant vocalized a desire for additional phases of the program or additional facets to allow participants to continue being a part of the program. An additional recommendation related to altering the meeting details to accommodate those with difficult work schedules or travel struggles.

Discussion

Recidivism

The staff at AMEND have been trying to educate judges and others in the local criminal justice system, telling them that treating anger management problems is not an effective way to prevent future intimate partner violence. Instead, programming based on the Duluth Model, which emphasizes personal responsibility and recognizing and controlling abusive behavior is assumed to be a much more effective preventive measure in this instance. This assertion by the AMEND staff is supported by the research literature (Day et al., 2009); though recent meta-analyses and other evaluations suggest that simply arresting perpetrators and letting them serve their time in the criminal justice system has similar results to all forms of intervention in terms of recidivism outcomes (Arias, et al., 2013; Herman, et al., 2014; Stover, et al., 2009).

The findings here seem to suggest – at least anecdotally – a positive recidivism outcome for AMEND program participants, though the sample size is small and geographically limited. Generally, completion of the AMEND program resulted in slightly lower recidivism rates and notably lower bail amounts. Also, the crimes reported by those who did not complete the AMEND program were more severe as indicated by bail amounts and types of crimes committed. Finally, the total days incarcerated were much higher for those who did not complete the AMEND program; this, in turn, led to an overall savings of $340.72 per person per day in incarceration costs and overall savings close to $15,000. This suggests the possibility of financial benefits accruing to the referring county when staff refers perpetrators to batterer intervention programs such as AMEND.

The findings here suggest that when traditional definitions of recidivism are used to assess program effectiveness there is less compelling evidence of effectiveness in reducing recidivism. However, a fiscal and cost-effectiveness perspective may provide local and state officials with a strong argument for the use of batterer intervention programs. The costs associated with such programs are certainly lower than the costs associated with the simple incarceration of perpetrators.

Group dynamics and program outcomes

The post-AMEND outcomes for the interviewees in this research reflect the potential for these programs to induce behavior change – and possibly long-term behavior change – for successful program participants. According to Gondolf (2004), men who receive treatment services for at least two months in batterer intervention programs are 50% less likely to re-assault than those men who do not receive treatment services.

All six interviewed participants agreed that they were happy with the fact that the group included other men going through similar situations. These connections to other similarly minded men allowed the participants to have someone they could relate to and go to for advice on how to prevent abusing their current or future partners. It appears that being around others who are dealing with similar situations, even for a short period, can allow a batterer to learn different ways to prevent future abuse from the other participants of the program.

The group dynamics of the AMEND program had a large impact on changes in participant accountability. Group members quickly learn that other members will challenge any statement that suggests that someone else is to blame for the participant's problems/challenges. This is intentional, but some of the benefits and the success of group dynamics cannot be planned. One interviewee mentioned the following about what is the most important factor in predicting success in the program: "the most is accountability, and least is accountability." In other words, accountability is the most important factor in predicting successful completion of the AMEND program; and if a participant does not learn accountability then it becomes the most important factor in predicting the unsuccessful completion of the program. Thus, if the accountability in the group did not challenge the participants, it would not be a successful group that encourages change (Zastrow, 2012). The enforcement of personal accountability through group dynamics is ultimately what works to change the participants and encourages the participants to let the AMEND program work for them.

Future research and implications for practice

Because of the seriousness of Intimate Partner Violence as a social justice issue affecting millions of women and children across the globe (NASW, 2018), every possible means must be employed to prevent and end such violence. Batterer Intervention programs such as the AMEND program described here serve both to reduce intimate partner violence with each participant who completes such a training. A primary purpose of this project was to assess the AMEND program and to lay the groundwork for the application for further funding for a long-term three to five-year follow-up study of the AMEND program. Such research might confirm, or ideally contrast with recent large-scale studies and Meta-analyses that show mediocre outcomes at best for these batterer intervention programs (Stover, et al., 2009). Ultimately, the goal of this work and research is to change the thinking of the courts and social service providers when dealing with perpetrators of intimate partner violence. Such perpetrators would then ideally be referred to rehabilitative batterer intervention programs rather than less effective anger management programs or simple arrest, incarceration, and release. Programs presented through group work can be effective due to the group dynamics at play and the influence of group members on each other. These changes in the sentencing and treatment of perpetrators have the potential to positively impact the lives of many victims across the globe by reducing the future incidence and impact of intimate partner violence.

References

Aguirre, R. P., Lehmann, P., & Patton, J. D. (2011). A Qualitative Look at the Perceived Strengths of Male Batterers: Implications for Intervention Programs. *Journal of Family Social Work, 14*(2), 125–143. doi:10.1080/1 0522158.2011.548138

AMEND (n.d.) AMEND an educational program for men who abuse/batter. [handout]

Arias, E., Arce, R., & Vilariño, M. (2013). Batterer intervention programmes: A meta-analytic review of effectiveness. *Psychosocial Intervention, 22*(2), 153–160.

Breiding, M. J., Basile, K. C., Smith, S. G., Black, M. C., & Mahendra, R. R. (2015). *Intimate partner violence surveillance: Uniform definitions and recommended data elements*, Version 2.0. Atlanta (GA): National Center for Injury Prevention and Control, Centers for Disease Control and Prevention.

Corey, M. S., Corey, G., & Corey, C. (2018). *Groups. Process and practice.* Boston: Cengage.

Day, A., Chung, D., O'Leary, P., & Carson, E. (2009). Programs for men who perpetrate domestic violence: an examination of the issues underlying the effectiveness of intervention programs. *Journal of Family Violence, 24*(3), 203–212.

Gondolf, E. W. (2004). Evaluating batterer counseling programs: A difficult task showing some effects and implications. *Aggression and Violent Behavior, 9*(6), 605–631.

Herman, K., Rotunda, R., Williamson, G., & Vodanovich, S. (2014). Outcomes from a Duluth Model Batterer Intervention Program at completion and long term follow-up. *Journal of Offender Rehabilitation, 53*(1), 1–18.

National Association of Social Workers (NASW). (2018). *Social Justice Brief: Social Work's Role in Responding to Intimate Partner Violence.* Washington, DC.

Pence, E. & Paymar, M. (1993). *Education groups for men who batter: The Duluth Model.* New York: Springer.

Powell, P. & Smith, M. (2011). *Domestic Violence: An Overview.* University of Nevada Cooperative Extension.

Price, B. J. & Rosenbaum, A. (2009). Batterer intervention programs: A report from the field. *Violence & Victims, 24*(6), 757–770.

Scott, M. & Easton, C. (2010). Racial differences in treatment effect among men in a substance abuse and domestic violence program. *The American Journal of Drug and Alcohol Abuse, 36*, 357–362.

Solinas-Saunders, M. & Thaller, J. (2015). The Use of Batterer Intervention Programs for Domestic Violence Offenders: An Assessment of Cognitive Accountability Training. *Journal of Community Corrections, 25*(1), 7–21.

Stover, C. S., Meadows, A. L., & Kaufman, J. (2009). Interventions for intimate partner violence: Review and implications for evidence-based practice. *Professional Psychology: Research and Practice, 40*(3), 223–233.

Tollefson, D. R., Webb, K., Shumway, D., Block, S. H., & Nakamura, Y. (2009). A mind-body approach to domestic violence perpetrator treatment: program overview and preliminary outcomes. *Journal of Aggression, Maltreatment & Trauma, 18*(1), 17–45.

Toseland, R. W. & Rivas, R. F. (2012) *An Introduction to Group Work Practice.* (7th ed.). Boston: Allyn & Bacon.

Truman, J., L. & Morgan, R., E. (2014). *Nonfatal Domestic Violence, 2003–2013.* U.S. Department of Justice. www.ojp.usdoj.gov (2)

Ventura, L., Lambert, E., White, T., & Skinner, K. (2007). Women and men in jail: attitudes towards and experiences of domestic violence. *American Journal of Criminal Justice, 31*, 37–48.

Zastrow, C. H. (2012). *Social Work with Groups: A comprehensive worktext.* (8th ed.). Belmont: Thomson Brooks/Cole.

Populism:
A challenge for groupwork

Jennie Fleming and Dave Ward

Introduction

Populism is currently a very fashionable term in political discourse but as we will explore later it has a long and complex history. Nowadays, Populism is widely linked with Donald Trump's ascendency to the presidency in the USA, Brexit in the UK, Marine Le Pen's challenge in France, Duterte's brutal regime in the Philippines, to name a few. It reflects a resurgence of the will of an erstwhile excluded section of the citizenry, newly inspired, energised and empowered to ensure that their self-defined needs and interests are considered and met by national leaders and governments.

This description resonates uncannily with the democratic values espoused by groupwork (Abels & Garvin, 2010) and, especially those of self-directed and social action groupwork (Mullender, Ward & Fleming, 2013). Is this an issue for groupworkers? If so, what do we need to consider; what might we do? In this paper, we are looking to stimulate deliberation and debate rather than provide answers.

Up to now, we would argue, a fundamental concern for groupworkers has been to counter the individualization of problems and solutions through which "public issues" have been translated into "personal troubles" (Wright Mills, 1970). This has involved laying at the door of the individual the responsibility for the problems they face and so rendering the policies of governments, and the behaviour of organisations and institutions, beyond scrutiny and unaccountable for these problems. This process can leave people divided from one another, blaming themselves and isolated from those who share similar experiences (Fook, 2002 cited in Trevithick, 2005, p. 84).

Reinforcing these processes, we have seen, increasingly, the development of educational and occupational cultures which are more and more top-down and prescriptive, preoccupied with following rules, performance indicators and output measures (Pullen Sansfacon & Ward, 2014). The effect of these is a narrowing of vision, driving out of initiative and creativity, the generation of conformism and reluctance to question received ideas (Faulkner, 1995). For the individual, Sennett (2007) describes how, in the modern economy, only a certain kind of human being can prosper in unstable, fragmentary social conditions. They must manage short term relationships; develop new skills rapidly, as demands of the work setting shift, and let go of the past. In other words, Sennett states, people need to be able to discount experiences they have already had, resembling, in many respects, the persona of the consumer, an individual ever avid for new things. Like Sennett, groupworkers would say that most people are not like this: they need a sustaining and creative life narrative, they take pride in being good at something specific and they value the experiences that they have lived through and, above all, interaction with their fellows.

How then do we interpret the broadcast evidence (and our personal experience) of populist rallies, their displays of group energy and cohesiveness, of consciousness of the issues confronting the participants? This includes their holding governments – said to be in league with out-of-reach multi-national commercial interests – as responsible for job losses and the social and economic poverty of specific communities and the consequent impoverishment and detachment of people individually and collectively? To dismiss these groupings with references to the Nazi Nuremberg assemblies is not adequate; many of the understandings and aspirations revealed are ones which, in their work, groupworkers would have welcomed.

Populism explored

In an article written before the prominence of the populist events noted above, Cas Mudde (2015) highlighted the electoral success of left-wing populist parties such as Syriza in Greece and Podemos in Spain. Until then he noted that populism was almost exclusively linked to the far right, leading to a conflation of populism with xenophobia and intolerance, and the assertion that it reflects a re-emergence of fascism albeit in a different guise.

Federico Finchelstein (2017) seeks to disentangle the relationship of populism to fascism describing populism as a "recalibration of fascism for democratic times" (p. xxvi). He suggests populism reflects a singular and homogenising, anti-pluralistic ideology, distinguishing between friend and enemy and featuring a charismatic leader and identification with an idealised nation. Yet, unlike the fascism of Nazi Germany, Mussolini's Italy and Mosley's Blackshirts in the UK, contemporary populism allows for electoral politics so that, although not dictatorship, there is an intolerant and illiberal democracy that "lurks behind populism." (Selk, 2018, p. 680).

However, rather alarmingly, Finchelstein suggests that, at least in its right-wing form, populism is becoming more intolerant and is regaining some of the characteristics typical of fascism. In its post Second World War form, with leaders such as Peron in Argentina and, later, Berlusconi in Italy, Finchelstein argues that populism rejected the political violence and genocidal racism of fascism but, he says, "it is not the same with Trump, Salvini, Orban and Bolsanaro and other new populist caudillos of the present. Racism has again become of key importance (although) enemies of populism are not fully persecuted or eliminated as the enemies of fascism were" (pp. xxvi–xxvii).

The consensus among European elites (those with the most wealth and status in society) on the left and right has been that populism is inherently bad, dismissed as a "pathology of democracy" or, as the American historian Richard Hofstadter wrote in the 1960's, "the paranoid style of politics." The rise of left-wing populist movements and parties saw some shift in the public debate conceding that populism might have something to say to current democratic politics.

Although it is the rise of the populist right that overwhelmingly dominates attention and discourse, another contemporary commentator, Thomas Frank (2018) aims at what he calls the "devil" theory. Frank points out that historians trace the populist tradition in America back to the late 19th Century when a radical left-wing political party called Populist swept much of the USA. Populism in its 1890's permutation represented a vision of democratic participation. Far from being a threat to democracy, Populism was then characterised as a highpoint of democracy. Protest movements within this tradition have come and gone ever since then, for example, the anti-Vietnam War movement in the 1960's and Occupy Wall Street more recently.

Frank argues that Populism's evil right-wing "doppelganger" re-emerged in the late 1960's when Richard Nixon and George Wallace worked out how to turn the language of working-class aspirations and discontents against liberalism, opening the door to the triumph of business over rivals such as the trade unions and the regulatory state. Thus, Frank argues, liberal democracy is now under threat not as a result of "unmodified populism" but as a result of the rise of neoliberalism over the last 40 years which he says dwarfs and subsumes populist leaders such as Trump. Indeed, he claims the correct name for Trump's politics is "demagoguery" or "pseudo-populism."

For Mudde (2004) populism is represented in the notion of "thin-centered ideology." By this, he suggests that expressions of populism are almost always combined with quite different (thin and full) ideologies, such as conservatism, liberalism, nativism, or "Americanismo." This implies that in the real world there are few, if any, pure forms of populism (in isolation) but, rather, subtypes of it, which show a specific articulation of certain ideological features.

In this vein, writing about the rise of the populist Front National in France, Eribon (2009) argues the responsibility of a left which ended up abandoning the "working class" as a political concept, anchored in the labour movement, through which people could experience fellow feeling with others in the same boat. With the turn in the 80's and 90's, by the left as well as the right, towards a focus on individual rights and responsibilities, he says this idea of group feeling was atomised into the responsibilisation of individuals (Liebenberg, Ungar & Ikeda, 2015) (for example, regarding social service responses to disadvantaged young people) and, in times of austerity, the scapegoating of marginal sections of the population.

What gained ground to take its place was a cynical fermentation and exploitation of anti-immigrant attitudes by the far-right which brought the working class back together but this time under a mood of hostile nativism rather than economic solidarity. No longer anchored to socialism and collectivism through the institutions of the labour movement such as trade unions and workers' education, the Front National populist party was able to present itself to be the only party that cared about them.

The currently dominant and strident right-wing breed of populism characterises society to be ultimately separated into two homogenous and antagonistic groups: "the pure people" versus "the corrupt elite," and postulates that politics should be an expression of the "will of the people" (Mudde, 2004).

Developing this analysis, Goodhart (2017) presents a separation in a society based on a division between the "Anywheres" and "Somewheres." The Anywheres, he argues, is only about 20–25%

of the population but their progressive individualist values and policies, prioritising openness, autonomy, and equal opportunities, have dominated politics and culture for more than a generation. In contrast, Somewheres, around half of the population, are people who value stability, familiarity, and more parochial group attachments and generally do not thrive in aspirational and meritocratic driven economies.

Goodhart (2017) argues that Somewheres and Anywheres do not know each other because so many able, ambitious people invariably feel they must leave their hometown to live an achieved life. This has come to be reflected in the split in England in the 2016 Brexit referendum between the metropolitan cities, London in particular, which voted Remain whereas a majority in the remainder of the country, composed of rural and, particularly, post-industrial urban communities voted to Leave, a phenomenon similar to the US election of Trump. Goodhart (2017) argues that both Anywhere and Somewhere worldviews are decent and legitimate, and it is the task of "politics" to find a settlement in which both groups feel their interests are respected.

Excavating these world views more deeply, Davies (2018), develops a concept he calls National Populism and proposes a taxonomy based on Four Ds: distrust of elites, destruction of national culture, economic deprivation, dealignment of political identification. These disadvantages, he says, are then countered by the reassertion by right-wing populists of:

- the need to preserve "cherished" national identities over rootless and diffuse transnational ones;
- the importance of stability and conformity over never-ending and disruptive instability that flows from globalisation and rapid ethnic change;
- the "will of the people" over that of elitist liberal metropolitan democrats who appear increasingly detached from the life experiences and outlooks of the so-called average citizen.

However, Davies is concerned that National Populism is only really distinguished from nationalism and racism by the fact that supporters do not see themselves in these terms. Driving a wedge between racism and a novel concept of "racial self-interest," discrimination for national populism is not racist if it is to simply to defend the broad parameters of the ethnic base of a country and its national identity. In such ways, right-wing populists try to build lost homelands. Heroic pasts are exaggerated or even fabricated. Everyone's motives are questioned so that no one can be trusted. Newspapers, politicians, judges, experts all have agendas, all are biased. It becomes best to have a strong hand to guide you (Bloomfield, 2019).

The main "good" of populism is that it brings to the fore the issues that large parts of the population care about, but that the political elites want to avoid discussing; think about immigration for the populist right or austerity for the populist left; how leaders from different parties can collude to keep issues that divide their respective electorates off the agenda – such as European integration and immigration.

The main "bad" of populism is that it denies the legitimacy of divisions of interests and opinions and rejects the integrity of opponents. As the populists are the voice of the people, anyone with a different view is said to speak for "special interests," even labelled as one of the "corrupt" elites. This uncompromising stand leads to a polarised culture, in which non-populists are turned into anti-populists.

Indeed, Mudde (2015) observes that populism tends to get "ugly" when it gets into power. History, he says, has shown that populists regularly have tried to circumvent or undermine the power of counterbalancing forces, including independent judges and the political opposition, including the introduction of new constitutions that significantly undermine the checks and balances of liberal democracy. The opposition is frustrated by a combination of legal and extra-legal pressures. In the end, Mudde (2015) argues, populism is an illiberal democratic response to undemocratic forces within liberalism. Rightly, it criticises the exclusion of important issues from the political agenda by the elites and calls for their repoliticisation. However, populism's inflexible views and uncompromising stand lead to a polarised society, denies legitimacy to opponents' opinions and weakens the rights of minorities. Furthermore, Runciman (2019) contends, the paradox of populist leaders is that they promise to empower the people but end up accumulating more and more power in their own hands. They undermine the authority of the democratic offices that they hold at the same time as exaggerating it. They are not testing the limits of their power: they are testing the limits of democracy itself.

With these understandings of populism in mind, there is surely a distinctive role for groupwork within its time-honoured purposes (Abels & Garvin, 2010). Nevertheless, perhaps there is a need for a serious rethink and regroup if we are to navigate an ethical yet practical path through "the good, the bad and the ugly" of 21st-century populist realpolitik. In the next section, we will consider a particular model of groupwork – Self-directed Groupwork and explore how it might offer a response to populism.

Social Action/Self-directed Groupwork

We have written extensively about the models of Self-directed Groupwork and Social Action (Mullender, Ward & Fleming, 2013) and there are numerous examples of the models in practice in books and journals (see for example *Groupwork* and Fleming and Ward, 2019). Therefore, we will not go into too much detail here, but give a brief overview of social action to understand how it can have a role in engaging with populism.

Social Action/Self-Directed Groupwork recognises the interwoven nature of personal and structural power relations as shown in the struggles of the black, feminist, LGBTQ and disability movements. Those who have engaged in these struggles have shown the complex way in which, intersectionally, the various dimensions of disadvantage and exclusion are distinctive but still interlink. Within the Self-directed Groupwork process, we see an approach that can achieve change and transformation at both levels, personal and structural. (See Fleming & Ward, 2017, for a more detailed exposition of theoretical foundations.)

This practice has been pursued in a multiplicity of settings across the world, with a range of participant groups, and by different professional disciplines and, not least, by volunteers, peers, patients, young people, carers, and users of services themselves. This reflects the genesis of the model as one which bridged professional and theoretical disciplines. It was developed by social workers, community and faith group activists, volunteers, patients and users of services, students, community workers, youth workers, teachers, health visitors, paid and unpaid carers, and others, drawing the best of each and from groupwork skills and concepts. They shared a grounding in certain practice principles that provided a common value base in which social action, as an evolving and reflexive praxis, grew.

Social Action and Self-directed Groupwork share much in common but are not entirely interchangeable. As practised in the UK, social action is a specific philosophy and theory for social change and provides a distinct form of practice for work in the full range of human services. It has been used in many different settings in countries across the globe. It is a truly international practice that can be tried and adapted for many different settings, for example, Fleming (2004) (Russia), Berden et al. (2006) (USA), Pullen Sansfacon et al. (2014) (Quebec), Boeck and Fleming (2019) (Peru). Self-directed groupwork, as a methodology for practice, lies at the core of Social Action.

Social Action/Self-directed Groupwork aims to empower group members. Social Action/Self-Directed Groupwork provides a distinctive way of working collectively to achieve empowerment. Crossing disciplinary boundaries, it mobilises the creativity, enthusiasm, and energy that emerge when people with similar interests, passions and experiences work together to achieve autonomous decision making and social action.

Social Action and Self-directed Groupwork combine two essential and inseparable elements: the six practice principles (see below) and a specific process. These are interdependent and the approach enables groups of all ages and circumstances to act and to achieve their collective goals. It offers an easy-to-understand and open-ended process that makes it possible for people to identify and act on issues that are important to them while working within a set of values which provide a clear and explicit value base.

A notable feature of the models is a clear value-base, which is outlined in the form of six practice principles, emphasising:

- the avoidance of negative labels,
- the rights of group members,
- basing intervention on a power analysis,
- assisting people to attain collective power through coming together in groups,
- group workers facilitating rather than leading,
- opposing oppression through practice and promoting social justice.

Inherent in these principles is an assumption of a social structural analysis of the issues facing marginalised groups and an over-arching commitment to social justice. However, considering the principle of promoting social justice through the lens of populism, does require that we ask, "Whose concept of social justice?" Taking Goodhart's (2017) definitions of Somewheres and Anywheres, everyone is an individual political being with their idiosyncratic mix of views and values. But we are also creatures of our circumstances and experiences, members of families, social groups, educational and ability categories, all of which leave their traces upon us in ways that we are often unaware of and incline us towards wider value groups. He suggests that these experiences lead to differing value clusters and therefore differing views on what is social justice.

Self-directed groups explicitly target external issues identified by group members through a process which involves them describing what is going on in their lives collectively and what are the major issues in their lives. They then consider why these issues exist. Next, the group thinks of how they might be able to take action to change things (a planning stage). They then undertake an agreed and planned course of action, following which the group together reflects on what has gone well, what has not, why, and how things could be done differently to move further towards their goal. As this description indicates, it is an iterative and cyclical process. Social Action groupworkers provide the framework for groups to consider problems, issues, and concerns. Group members provide the content, using their skills, knowledge, and expertise. Group members create the knowledge and understanding through active participation: describing, suggesting, analysing, deciding, experiencing and reflecting (Ward & Mullender, 1991). This process closely parallels the group-centred approach to social change developed by Paulo Freire (1972), which sets out three key elements: dialogue, problematisation and conscientisation. "Problematisation" is what gives Freire's work and, also Self-directed/Social Action Groupwork, a distinctive critical and radical edge.

This distinctiveness can be represented by the asking of the question "why?" are things this way. Asking "why?" directs the spotlight away from people as problems, on to the problems they encounter. This enables them to see opportunities to develop a wider range of options for action and change. This enables group members to understand new explanations in the wider social, political, and economic context and consider how they can identify and engage with these to bring about meaningful improvement in their everyday lives. Asking the question "why?" is the key that unlocks the process and is critical for a practice to be truly empowering (Mullender, Ward & Fleming, 2013).

"Why?" is the watchword of Social Action and provides the glue to cement the values into the practice. It sets Social Action apart from other practices, which often jump from the question "what?" to the question "how?" without considering the question "why?" in between. If this is not done, explanations, responsibilities and the scope of solutions are unwittingly steered to the private world around people and within their existing knowledge and experience. These have been fashioned by their position in society and the processes which keep them there. In asking "why?" people are encouraged to pursue an issue until the root causes have been identified and exposed. Asking "why?" allows people to "examine the internal bridles and perceived powerlessness which underpin their sense of self and guide their actions in the world" (Young 1999, p. 88). It enables people to break out of what can be a demoralising and self-perpetuating narrowness of vision, introspection, and self-blame created by poverty, lack of opportunity and exclusion and the neoliberal emphasis on self-responsibility. With expanded horizons of what is possible, people envisage new explanations in the wider social, political, and economic context and consider how they can engage with these. Asking "Why?" directs the spotlight onto the problems people encounter and enables them to see opportunities to develop a wider range of options for action and change. Asking the question "why?" is the key that unlocks the process.

Grounded in sharing and partnership, group members come to possess and exhibit the values and the "imagination" (Wright Mills, 1970) to envision and reach out beyond the conventionally defined boundaries of their disciplines, work settings, and experiences. Experiencing this process as facilitators and participants, we have not found that group members arrive at "ugly" right-wing populist understandings and plans of action. Rather the opposite, the process not only leads to a structural understanding of problems but also provides an interpersonal experience which suggests personal relationships and interactions which are respectful, socially progressive and collaborative: in sum, embedded in notions of human rights and social justice, valuing each person for what they are. In essence: ubuntu.

Conclusion: Challenging populism through self-directed groupwork/social action

As groupworkers it is our ethical responsibility to challenge the "ugly" manifestation that is right-wing Populism. It is fundamental to our values and the nature and reality of our practice that we will need to start small. But we should not be deterred by that. Populism is an ideology but, as we have seen, as currently manifested in predominantly its right-wing form, it is not simply an abstract notion: it has real consequences at the local and personal levels. This is exactly where groupworkers operate and where they can engage with, challenge and, hopefully, begin to roll back some of the uglier manifestations of populism. Self-directed Groupwork /Social Action is to be one approach that can be used in this context.

Self-directed Groupwork requires engaging in an alternative progressive culture which has an established history, and which turns conventional processes on their head. Indeed, Finchelstein (2017) argues encouragingly that if we do this, we will be going along with the grain of history which, he says, "teaches us that a strong civil society can forcefully challenge populists in power" (p. xxxix).

In a widely accepted definition, the World Bank (2007) states that civil society refers to a wide array of organizations, ranging through social movements, community groups, non-governmental organizations, labour unions, indigenous groups, charitable organizations, faith-based organizations, professional associations, and foundations that have a presence in public life and express the interests and values of their members or others, based on ethical, cultural, political, scientific, religious or philanthropic considerations. It is in the non-governmental sector that many groupworkers operate and, as our examples will show, can be where, particularly if the principles and methods of Self-directed Groupwork/Social Action are to the fore, the tenets of populism may be challenged.

To recap, in Self-directed Groupwork/Social Action, the process comes first, with the confidence and expectation that "product" will emerge from this. Instead of planning and then involving, it means starting with engaging with people, working through their preconceived ideas with rigorous and persistent use of the question why? Having reached the core of the problem the group can move on to planning and action.

The term "Self-directed" emerged initially as simply descriptive of the activity in groups undertaking some form of social action – working to create change in their lives and communities – but which distinctively incorporated a primary focus on addressing a shared structural issue rather than meeting the individual needs of the participants, although of course, the latter may still happen. As referenced earlier, some such groups were based in and arose directly from a specific awareness of Self-directed Groupwork and others which, when we described the process and principles, immediately responded with "That is just what we do" and recognised the model in their work. Some groups and practices may not be aware of this terminology but demonstrate practices and methods which place them comfortably within the "family." To illustrate how Self-directed

Groupwork can work challengingly on the terrain of populism we will draw upon examples from this broad field.

Peter Westoby and colleagues (2019) report an Australian Project of Participatory Action Research Project "motivated by the painful political events and processes unfolding around the world in 2017" (p. 2207) within which populism was core. Using a framework grounded in the pedagogy of Paulo Freire (1972) and recognisably congruent with Self-directed Groupwork, working with some thirty social work practitioners, several new initiatives were implemented including the formation of a new Popular Education Network, through a process which combined learning, organising and linking to progressive social movements.

Less directly, there has been the burgeoning interest in Citizens' Assemblies as a method for finding a path forward on issues that profoundly split populations. Famously they were set up by the government and used in the run-up to the recent referenda in the Republic of Ireland on gay marriage and abortion. Their deliberations anticipated the outcomes of the referenda. However, interestingly, the British government refused to sponsor such a process in relation to the Brexit issue. It was taken up by several unofficial organisations in the non-governmental sector, but they received minimal attention in the rancorous debate of the time and, arguably, were drowned out by the populist rhetoric of the pro-Brexit lobby.

As set out by the Electoral Reform Society Ireland (2018), a Citizens' Assembly resonates strongly with the principles and practice of Self-directed Groupwork/Social Action. It is a form of deliberative democracy: a process through which citizens can engage in open, respectful and informed discussion and debate with their peers on a given issue. An assembly is composed of a chairperson and 99 ordinary citizens randomly selected to be "broadly representative of Irish society" in terms of age, gender, social class, and regional spread. The assemblies in question deliberated for five sessions. Members were given information on the topic, heard from experts, and reviewed written submissions from members of the public and interest groups. The members adopted key principles to guide their debate: the openness of proceedings; fairness in how differing viewpoints were treated; equality of voice among members; efficiency; respect; and collegiality.

A social action group facilitated by one of the authors met on school premises outside school hours. Its focus was on campaigning to improve youth facilities in the neighbourhood where the group members lived. The group had Black and White members, reflecting the multi-racial demography of the area. In the wider region, there is a strong and active National Front/British National Party presence. They had targeted this school among others for distributing anti-immigrant racist literature. Some of the young White people in the group initially found the Front's ideas appealing although they exempted Black group members: "They're our friends; they're different."

In group discussions the context and implications of the Front's ideas, rhetoric and practices were examined, setting them in the context of British colonial history and current economic, social, and political conditions and issues. Members manifestly deepened their understanding of the Front's ideology and purposes and even challenged the agitators at the school gate. Through such limited experiences, learning, and action we saw how it was possible to begin to challenge, in a real way, expressions of the "ugly" side of populism.

In an evaluation of another similar neighbourhood-based Social Action group (Mullender et al., 2013: pp. 135-136), the young people fed back to an independent researcher about the process through which such developments can take place:

> *By sitting down and talking and working it out together, you can solve the problem. You can't have one person going one way, and one another – you are not going to solve anything.*

> *I think we just learnt to communicate – that's what I think it is – talk – seriously, not loudly – not wind each other up. Brainwork – made us think.*

> *The thing was that it was mixed, there were black, white, Asian – it was a small estate and we were all together. We all stuck together – never let each other down. That still stands to this day.*

The self-directed process involves a double-sided value commitment: on one side, to push back against intolerant populism and forwards towards greater social justice; on the other, albeit pulled back by fear, reluctance, and conventional wisdom, to surrender and share power. The philosopher Slavoj Zizek (2017) suggests that, in the wider sphere, such a process can be seen in the increasing commitment of academics and artists to Creative Commons, to the freedom and exchange of the world wide web and, not least, in the infinite number and variety of "actes gratuits" that pass between people everywhere.

For some groupworkers the process may feel like a journey into the unknown but, once engaged in Self-directed/Social Action groupwork, paid workers, activists, researchers and managers can find that it is one that works. We hope we have encouraged and enabled people who have not yet taken the steps outlined above now to have the confidence to do so, to try it for themselves and challenge the ugly side of populism – and go on to make a difference!

References

Abels, P. & Garvin, C. (2010). *Standards for social work practice with groups* (2nd ed.). Alexandria (VA): Association for the Advancement of Social Work with Groups.

Boeck, T. & Fleming, J. (2019) Working with a women's group in Titilaka, Peru to form a knitting association: An example of value based groupwork. *Groupwork*, 28(3), 23-47

Bloomfield, S. (2019). Fake news creates confusion boosting hardline rulers and killing democracy, this timely study argues. (Review of P. Pomerantsev, This Is Not Propaganda: Adventures in the War Against Reality). *The Guardian Review*, 10/08/19, p. 23.

Davies, W. (2018). A defence of Brexit and Trump supporters, and of racial self-interest, claims to be myth-busting. Is it just wrong? (Review of R. Eatwell and M. Goodwin, National Populism: The Revolt Against Liberal Democracy). *The Guardian Review*, 17/11/18, p. 18.

Electoral Reform Society of Ireland (2018). *The Irish abortion referendum: How a Citizens' Assembly helped to break years of political deadlock.* Retrieved from https://www.electoral-reform.org.uk/the-irish-abortion-referendum-how-a-citizens-assembly-helped-to-break-years-of-political-deadlock/

Eribon, D. (2009). *Returning to Reims*, Los Angeles CA: Semiotext(e), reviewed in Steven Poole, A Virtuosic Account of childhood among a French working class that now seems to have deserted the left, *The Guardian Review*, 4/8/18, p. 14.

Faulkner, D. (1995). The Criminal Justice Act 1991: Policy, legislation and practice. in D. Ward and M. Lacey (Eds.) *Probation: Working for Justice.* London: Whiting and Birch.

Finchelstein, F. (2017). *From Fascism to Populism in History.* Berkeley, CA:

University of California Press.

Fleming, J. (2004). The beginning stages of a social action training event. *Groupwork, 14*(2), 24–41, reprinted in J. Fleming and D. Ward (Eds.) (2019). *Social Action and Self-directed Groupwork*, London: Whiting and Birch, 248–264.

Fleming, J. & Ward, D. (2013). Facilitation and groupwork tasks in self-directed groupwork. *Groupwork, 23*(2), 48–66.

Fleming, J. & Ward, D. (2017). Self-directed Groupwork – social justice through social action and empowerment. *Critical and Radical Social Work, 5*(1), 75–91.

Fleming, J. & Ward, D. (Eds.) (2019). *Social Action and Self-directed Groupwork*. London: Whiting and Birch.

Fook, J. (2002). *Social work: critical theory and practice*. London: Sage.

Frank, T. (2018). These books present populism as a new and powerful threat to liberal democracy. But what if they have got it all wrong? (Review of Y. Mounk, *The People vs Democracy: Why Our Freedom is in Danger and How to Save It* and of W. A. Galston, *Anti-Pluralism: The Populist Threat to Liberal Democracy*), *The Guardian Review*, 26/5/18, 12–13.

Freire, P. (1972). *Pedagogy of the Oppressed*. Harmondsworth: Penguin.

Goodhart, D. (2017). *The Road to Somewhere: The New Tribes Shaping British Politics*. London: C. Hurst & Co.

Hofstadter, R. (1964). *The Paranoid Style in American Politics: An Essay*, New York: Vintage.

Liebenberg, L., Ungar, M., & Ikeda, J. (2015). Neo-Liberalism and responsibilisation in the discourse of Social Service Workers. *British Journal of Social Work, 45*(3), 1006–1021.

Mudde, C. (2004). "The Populist Zeitgeist." *Government and Opposition, 39*(4), 541–63.

Mudde, C. (2015). Europe Opinion: The problem with populism, *The Guardian*. Retrieved from https://www.theguardian.com/commentisfree/2015/feb/17/problem-populism-syriza-podemos-dark-side-europe

Mullender, A., Ward, D., & Fleming, J. (2013). *Empowerment in Action: Self-directed Groupwork*. Basingstoke (UK): Palgrave.

Pullen Sansfacon, A. & Ward, D. (2014). Making Inter-professional working work: Introducing a Groupwork Perspective. *British Journal of Social Work, 44*(5), 1284 –1300.

Pullen Sansfacon, A., Ward, D., Dumais-Michaud, A-A., Robichaud, M-J., & Clegg, A. (2014). Working with parents of gender independent children: using social action as an emancipatory research framework. *Journal of Progressive Human Services, 25*(3), 214–219.

Runciman, D. (2019). Unlocking Power, *The Guardian Review*, 10/8/19, 10–15.

Sennett, R, (2007). *The Culture of New Capitalism*, New Haven: Yale University Press.

Selk, V. (2018). Book Review: From Fascism to Populism in History. *Constellations*, 25, 680–684.

Trevithick, P. (2005). The knowledge base of groupwork and its importance within social work. *Groupwork, 15*(2), 80–107.

Ward, D. & Mullender, A. (1991). Facilitation in Self-directed Groupwork. *Groupwork, 4*(2), 141–151, reprinted in J. Fleming and D. Ward (Eds.) (2019). *Social Action and Self-directed Groupwork*, London: Whiting and Birch, 172–184.

Westoby, P., Lathouras, A., & Shevellar, L. (2019). Radicalising community development within social work – a participatory action research project. *British Journal of Social Work, 49*(8), 2207–2225.

World Bank (2007). *Consultations with Civil Society*, Washington D.C.: Civil Society Team, World Bank.

Wright Mills, C. (1970). *The Sociological Imagination*, Harmondsworth: Penguin.

Young, K. (1999). "The Youth Worker as Guide, Philosopher and Friend" in S. Banks (Ed.) *Ethical Issues in Youth Work*, London: Routledge.

Zizek, S. (2017). *The Courage of Hopelessness: Chronicles of a Year of Acting Dangerously*, London: Penguin, cited in Self, W. (2017). The Courage of Hopelessness: how the big hairy Marxist would change the world. *The Guardian* 28th April 2017. Retrieved from https://www.theguardian.com/books/2017/apr/28/courage–of-hopelessness-slavoj-zizek-review

Using arts as a contact method in group work with latency age Arab and Jewish youth in Israel

Noa Barkai and Ephrat Huss

Introduction

One of the strategies of coping with the Arab-Israeli conflict on the educational and social level has involved attempts to bring together Jewish and Arab youth citizens of Israel. Beginning in the 1980's, many encounters have taken place in Israel, to influence mutual perceptions and improve relations between Jews and Arabs. While some places – regions, nations, towns, and villages manage to remain peaceful despite ethnic diversity others experience enduring patterns of violence. Research about conflicts around the globe has found that the missing link, which causes this difference, is closely related to inter-communal civic engagement. Civic engagement may lead to building more peaceful relations between communities and ethnic groups (Harel-Shalev, 2010). However, most of these groups are based on dialogue around self-identity and around the political problem, and so target older adolescents and young adults such as students, who can dialogue using more abstract concepts and narrative self-disclosure as a reflective method. However, latency aged children are less suited for this type of dialogue due to their more cognitive rather than emotional focus, and less abstract thinking. This also makes them hard candidates for group work that is not action focused. Additionally, the tension between individual and group is complex as much effort is put into fitting into a group at this age. This makes shifts in-group norms towards accepting the other, in a country in a direct conflict between groups, especially complicated at this age.

Additionally, difficulty in regulating behavior, in general, makes social responses of adolescents to complex social situations such as meeting the "other" more complex. However, in the Arab Israeli conflict, there is political violence already at the age of thirteen, with desperate violent acts of stabbing occurring at younger ages, the extreme violence and racism are typical of the rest of the world as well. It seems that we must find ways to utilize group work to address hate of the other, lower negative stereotypes and enhance complex understanding and empathy at an earlier age.

Based on the above use of group work with latency aged students, then Contact theories of meeting the other would seem most suitable for young adolescents who do not yet have the abstract skills to discuss conflicts on a high level. An action-based approach aiming at gaining familiarity, having good times together, and creating joint projects, rather than intense dialogues, seems a more developmentally appropriate method to create cooperation, friendship, and good neighboring.

In the following case study of an Arab Israeli youth group, we turned to the arts to create positive interaction based on joint activity between two groups of youth from conflicting communities, in this case, the Bedouin-Arab and Jewish youth of the Negev area in Israel. We envisioned that the project would enable broad and long-term inter-communal interaction based on the groups' common physical living area and that getting to know youth from the other group personally, would help to eliminate prevailing stereotypes and create a sense of joint ownership through contact.

In this study, we discuss the complexity of creating these meetings and their value as well as pitfalls, as a case study, to illuminate the methodological and theoretical dilemmas of such encounter groups with young adolescents. In this study, we wanted to ask what are the advantages and pitfalls of bringing together youth into action-based group work in conflict situations?

Our qualitative findings point to a complex picture – including both enhanced contact and fun on the immediate group level, and contact on the personal level, but also a continuation of stereotypes and continued discomfort with the other group as a group, even when individual friendships were created. Thus, the personal "fun" and connection, was not generalized to the political or ethnic level. This raises interesting questions about how to address racism, othering, and political contact in group work. It also raises questions about the use of "here and now contact" or action methods in group work. On a methodological level, it points to the need for qualitative evaluation of group work to understand complex clusters of findings that may seem oppositional.

Theories of encounters between youth in conflict groups

Currently, there is a wide range of studies on encounter groups between Jews and Arabs youth in Israel (Maoz, 2011). Over the past decade, several studies dealing with a qualitative assessment of the encounter groups have also been published, relating to description and analysis of the interaction processes that occur within the encounter, as well as to group dynamics, interpersonal connections formed in the groups, and emotions and reflections that the participants bring up as a result of the encounter. However, this is usually undertaken with older youth (Berger et al., 2015; Binder et al., 2009).

Biton and Salomen (2006) examined a variety of peace education programs in the world, among them encounter groups, and noted an overall minority of assessments; Maoz (2011) comprehensively investigated Jewish-Arab encounter programs based on the confrontation model, attempted to define several assessment criteria, emphasizing the establishment of the encounter experience over time; the quality of relations created between the group participants; the capacity to reduce the inherent asymmetry; and the capability to define goals and fulfill them. Katz and Mayah (1990) claim that, in light of the conflict's complexity and the multiple dilemmas that arise in designing and conducting the encounter groups, perhaps a process of clarification of the goals for the individual participant should replace the delineation of unambiguous and universal objectives.

The researchers suggest that an understanding of the dilemmas resting on the foundation of the encounter can be an objective in itself and that the role of the encounter is not to instantaneously solve dilemmas in the external reality, but to assist in participants' overall comprehension and to offer possible tools for coping. Sagi, 2002, has studied encounter groups of various types and has asserted that, when the groups involved are in protracted conflict, there is a need for a "good enough" model of educational activities, and one cannot expect too many successes.

The research literature presents three primary models of encounters between groups in conflict. The encounter model, developed at the Neve Shalom School of Peace as a response to criticism of the Contact Hypothesis, focuses on collective identity and the asymmetrical power relations between the parties, at the expense of lessening the opportunity to create personal connections among the participants (Ben Asher at al., 2020). The purpose of this strategy is to empower the minority group and help the dominant group cope with ambivalence and conflicts surrounding control and domination. Studies have shown that the advantage here lies in the propensity of the participants to engage in internal work and to attempt to cope with the difficult subjects that arise within the encounters. The main drawback regards the difficulty of the external – and sometimes internal – struggle, and the frustration experienced at times when the participants return to life outside of the workshop and the perpetuation of the power asymmetries to which they related within the encounter meetings This model demands the reflective skills that are absent at the time of late latency and adolescence and so we did not use this model for our group. The second model is the life-storytelling model: A relatively new methodology, the purpose here is integrating the two preceding models. Participants from both sides share with the group their family stories, which they have collected by interviewing family members from two generations. The mutual storytelling allows and encourages a personal connection, as well as a discussion of the collective components of the stories (for example, the Holocaust for the Jews and the 1948 Al-Naqba catastrophe for the Arabs). Through the stories, in-depth personal and group work on the topics tied to the conflict is made possible. As the life story model is a relatively new method, there have been very few attempts to assess it as such. Studies have shown the potential of this approach to stimulate the ability and willingness to develop familiarity and acquaintanceship between the two groups, to listen to each other, and to create mutual awareness and empathy toward the "other" (Steinberg & Bar-On, 2002; Brown & Hewstone, 2005). This method could be attempted with our age group, but it is not clear that the youth can gather and address the family narrative from an emotional standpoint, as it is often very flooding.

The third model, based primarily on the Contact Hypothesis (Pettigrew & Tropp, 2011), the central objective is the creation of personal relationships between the participants, under the assumption that through personal acquaintanceship it is possible to prevent and change stereotypic perceptions, attitudes, and behavior. In these encounters, there is little discussion of the historical background and the current political realities of the groups. Studies have shown that this approach has short-term advantages but fewer long-term advantages, as in most cases the hostile political and/or historical reality eradicates the beneficial effect of the interpersonal connection (Maoz, 2011). This was felt to be most relevant for late latency and early adolescence, based on the literature on this developmental stage above: The foundation of this project and research is based on "contact theory" which emphasized the sense of social equality which has to occur for acquaintance programs to be successful. Four prerequisite features are important for contact to be successful at reducing intergroup conflict and achieving intergroup harmony. First, equal status within the contact situation second, intergroup cooperation third, shared common goals and finally support of authorities, law, or custom (Pettigrew & Tropp, 2011). All these elements have been incorporated into the project design of our meetings between Jewish and Bedouin youth.

An important factor for the development of intergroup friendships is the opportunity for personal acquaintance between the members. The youth groups undertaken in our study were based on joint positive experienced created through games, and through new cooking, arts, and sports experienced together.

Studies have found that people with out-group friends had significantly lower levels of bias toward the group and these people play a critical role in their inner group to reduce bias and negative feelings towards the other group (Here & Capitanio, 1996; Pettigrew & Tropp, 2011). Thus, during encounters and meetings if members of two groups are teamed from an outside source it is good, however, if they choose each other as partners on an assignment this could be the greatest success. It should be noted that when personalization occurs with those whose characteristics do not support stereotypic expectations it enhances positive contact and reduces stigmatization (Bar-Tal & Rosen, 2009). As a result of positive intergroup interaction within the contact situation development of new norms of intergroup acceptance that can be generalized to new situations and attitudes toward the out-group can be facilitated. Moreover, a favorable intergroup contact leads to psychological processes that reduce dissonance and produce more favorable attitudes toward individuals from the other group or/ and toward the group as a whole for these perceptions to be consistent with the positive nature of the interaction. A dissonance reduction can also serve as a justification of the interaction with the other group and as a result, positive behavioral interactions may induce greater intergroup acceptance Furthermore, not only attitudes can be changed but intergroup contact, but the interaction can also enhance empathy toward members of the other group (Brown & Hewstone, 2005).

Latency and early adolescents in groups

Adolescence is a period of growth and development between childhood and adulthood. This developmental period involves new demands on the individual. A major task of this period is moving towards independence from dependency on the family, therefore peers become a crucial socialization circle for the adolescent (Erikson, 1982; Flum, 1994). Adolescents have difficulty in social cues during challenging situations, due to their difficulty in regulating behavior in general that make social responses of adolescence to complex social situations such as meeting the "other" more complicated and based on emotion rather than on a rational response. At the same time, this age is a particularly important developmental stage, since social, emotional, and cognitive processes are involved in the attempts to navigate these increasingly complex relationships. Indeed, it is during these years that abstract thinking and cognitive processing develops along with enhanced moral reasoning and judgment. These positive processes enable the adolescent to explore the world, gain competences, and contribute to the world surrounding him/her (Binder et al. 2009).

Arts as action methods in group work

The arts are a deep and universal psycho-neurological construct through which people process their experiences. They are central to human functioning, contributing to the individual's sense of self, and to the ability to remain oriented in the world and to pursue goals effectively in light of memories of the experience and future problem solving based on them (Huss, 2012, 2013; Hickson & Barker, 2002).

The use of arts in conflict as a form of contact activity and as an indirect transitional space within which to structure interactions is discussed in the art therapy literature. A multi-model arts theory claims that art processes enable joint interaction and "doing" within a safe symbolic space that enables structured interaction and the creation of a joint product that demonstrates this. These processes also create a concrete product as documentation of the possibility of working together and creating new products within a group context, the artworks are experienced as a jointly created image that becomes a jointly owned recourse that connects all of the viewers (Ben-Ezer, 2002; Benson, 1987; Docker, 1998; Dewey, 1934).

The arts are also utilized within conflict groups as a way to learn the central symbols and cultural beliefs of the other in a safe non-confronted area such as decoration and cooking that are less space that encourages empathy and a meeting on a basic universal level. Cooking, crafts, and music are often used to enhance empathy and identification within conflict and forgiveness groups. In reconciliation activities, learning about and creating traditional craft activities together is also cited as a way of distancing differences to a non-threatening arena (Kalmanovich & Lloyd, 2005).

In latency, art tends to be product and action-oriented, rather than as a trigger for a personal narrative and self-reflection (Huss, 2012, 2015). We incorporated this into the above uses of arts; additionally, latency youth are especially culturally invested in the technology of visual images. This enables them to define their joint youth-culture symbols as organizing metaphors for identity.

Research methods

This paper will use a multiple case study frame of four encounter-based mixed groups of Bedouin-Arab and Jewish youth, who met for a year with ten meetings for each group. The encounters took place in alternative places, in each of the Bedouin or Jewish communities as well as in neutral places such as the university. The encounters included a variety of action-based activities and structured interaction games based on the above literature. This included learning about each other's community, learning about and making traditional foods and holidays, outdoor challenge activities, arts activities such as crafts, skills, and creating a joint Facebook page. The encounters took place as extra-curricular after school activity in four neighboring communities. Recruitment took place in schools for the Bedouin-Arab adolescents and via youth workers in the Jewish community. Masters students in the conflict management and resolution program led the encounters as Arab and Jewish co-leaders in each group. They had ongoing supervision for leading the groups.

Research strategy: The qualitative components of this research strategy will be described in this paper: They included observation and transcriptions as well as summarizing discussions with the participants. Observation is important because it enables the leaders to show how the youth interacted on non-verbal as well as verbal levels (Denzin & Lincoln, 2000).

The data sources included transcriptions of 30 meetings and photography of all artwork and activities of the meetings.

Analytical strategy: The qualitative data were analyzed on two levels. Firstly, the transcripts were analyzed narratively as a process, with each of the authors analyzing a different group over the twelve meetings. This enabled the authors to see developments and progressions within specific groups and about the group over time.

Reliability and validity: Reliability and validity were created through peer analyses of authors and triangulation of the qualitative methods including observation and interviews (Huberman & Miles, 2002).

Ethical issues: Because of the political climate in Israel, taking part in a mixed group can be stigmatizing and met with disapproval from peers and adults: This was overcome by maintaining anonymity in all materials published: Any images of participants received permission by the participants before showing. Additionally, the research received clearance from the university's Ethics Committee. Each of the parents signed a consent form to approve the documentation for his/her child (Huberman & Miles, 2002).

Presentation of the data and discussion

The data divides into two central themes: The first theme shows how the arts-based contact theory worked to create unity in these groups, and the second theme shows the limitations of that unity.

Contact theory: Themes connecting to "doing" together

Using games and activities that mix the groups: The contact theory was constructed around joint assignments using mixed groups and competition between the groups. The rules of the interactions were used as a model for cooperation as in the following example:

"A stick game that demands balance – you have to balance yourself, and then you have to check what is happening with everyone else, and help them reach balance – so that you will all stay in balance and each child can walk on the sticks, you have to notice what is happening to each child, and to hold the sticks together in a way that he won't fall."

Focusing on shared global youth-culture: Focusing on shared global youth-culture such as favorite singers, the children interacted about this easily and exchanged Facebook addresses and showed each other films of their favorite singers. This created lively discussions and inter-group cooperation.

Re-mixing of sub-groups: Remixing of sub-groups to create as much contact between groups as possible as the third way of creating contact was to demand constant mixing of the groups and to structure the time so that the children did not go back to their groups of origin but were in constant interaction with both groups.

These three methods produced a lot of observed contact and interaction between the two groups as in the following examples:

Five children, (2 Jewish and three Arab) discuss what to put on their collage-poster. They sit around it, talking, cutting, and sticking things. They plan a strategy that some will stay sitting and stick the new pictures, while others go to find more pictures. The sticking and finding groups were mixed Arab-Jewish

.

Yosef (Arab) finds a picture of himself and cuts it out. Muhamad (Arab) finds a picture in which Ofer (Jewish) is present and gives it to her to stick. She smiles, and he gets up to bring her scissors to cut the picture and stick it in the collage.

Yosef, Ofer, Muhamad, and Hassam are sticking pictures that they gathered together inside the areas that they colored with paint. The boys are very active around Ofer (girl). Muhamad sticks a picture of Ofer in the center and covers elements around her in white paint. He writes her name next to the picture in blue on white.

In the end, all the groups observed the posters, and each (mixed) group boasted that their poster was best.

Maintenance of contact beyond the limits of the group: The question arises if this interaction would be maintained over time, outside of the shared activities? We saw that the youth learned each other's names and exchanged Instagram and Facebook details. We saw a reduction in the number of stigmas that were verbalized at the beginning, as in the following examples:

One Jewish child started the meetings with a fear that the Arab children would smell bad, and fear of going on an Arab bus, but by the end of the meetings, she had a good Arab friend and was not scared of the bus. She also initiated cooperation with the Arab girls in a joint game.

One Arab boy, who only stood on the side in the first meetings, became regularly active and interactive with the Jewish boys on making a joint Facebook page in one of the meetings.

Cultural differences: Although the youth group is voluntary and so by definition the participants on both sides come from families with a peace-oriented outlook, and from relatively similar educated and middle-class families, there were still many cultural differences. Arab children were shocked by the lack of respect of the Jewish children to the adults and the Jewish children were shocked that an Arab child at a visit to his home, shouted at his dog.

Similarly, the addressing of the differences in their villages, through meeting consecutively in the Jewish, and then Arab village (as compared to meeting in the neutral ground such as the university) raised issues of asymmetry between the social realities of the two groups. The Jewish children were from the middle-class settlement, with many more financial recourses, while the Bedouin children were from the poorer settlement, in terms of size of houses, green areas, and more. The Jewish children had many extracurricular activities and could not find time to fit in meetings, whereas the Arab children had fewer meetings.

Difficulty with violent outbursts that created distrust on one occasion, as is typical in the south of Israel was a challenge. There was a violent outburst in the area and parents were scared to send their children to the meetings on both sides, so there was a break. The parents were terribly angry about what had happened (a killing and retaliation) and the group leaders tried to discuss this with the children when they did meet, but the children did not want to listen.

Another cultural difference was manifested in gender roles, with the Arab girls keeping away from all boys and the Jewish girls feeling free to interact with the Jewish and Arab boys. These differences were also "shown" on the level of behavior, for example, in non-formal time, when they were not placed together, they separated into their original groups and did not mix, or when the group made festive cookies of both Jewish and Arab group members, together, in mixed groups, they separated back into original groups with their cookies in break time.

Limitations of the unity

Overall inability to address ethnic and political differences: Another question is if this interaction enabled to touch upon conflicts and differences, that is, to move into the conflict stages of the group? We saw that whenever the youth leaders, based on the assumption that there was enough contact, did try to address differences, then the group refused to cooperate as in the following examples:

> One Arab girl described how she had a room with three other sisters, and a Jewish girl said she would die if she had to live with her sister in the same room. The Arab girl said that she liked their being together. They did not manage to continue the conversation.

> The group leaders asked a child from each group to describe their festivals and food in their favorite festival, and the other group could not sustain listening.

> The dominance of Hebrew over the Arabic language was also maintained in the artwork:

> Salam does another part of the poster and writes that Rahim and Rabat boys are best friends forever. He sticks pictures of the group as a whole and signed his name with a red star in English and Hebrew. No one writes in Arabic on the poster.

Summary and discussion

We see in the themes above, that while having fun and interacting together worked on the immediate and interpersonal level, it seems that the core differences – including the differences in culture, class and the social power – between Arab and Jewish youth as a collective group, were not influenced by the pleasant contact in the group.

It seems that the collective elements were disconnected from the personal elements. This is true also in adult society, where one can personally like someone from a different ethnic group but still maintain stereotypes and conflict with the group. Similarly, the action methods created "fun" and cooperation on an embodied level, but it seems that this needs to be taken further to address conflicts on the verbal level, also in Latency age groups that are not always open to discuss abstract concepts such as racism. This is a challenge. It could be that separate meetings to discuss experiences of the "other" would have helped to process these differences. However, the difficulty of finding youth that even agreed to come to these meetings was so intense because of the challenge of putting Arab and Jewish youth together at this age, that the youth leaders were invested in keeping the groups together, through action methods and through making them "fun" enough to attract the youth. This did not enable us to address the issues of conflict and move the group into the working stages. This orientation can also be understood as connected to the focus on "fun" in the way youth are educated in this era. This together with the difficulty in bringing them together in a time of extreme conflict in the south, makes it difficult to challenge the youth enough to address conflicts.

On this level, we can say that the action methods have a danger of becoming a way to stay stuck in the honeymoon stages of group work (Benson, 1987). At the same time, as in all group work, we cannot know the long-term impact of this meeting, and "having fun together" may influence these youth in the future.

The overall conclusion from this study is that while action methods did create personal contact and long term connections, and as such is useful in political conflict meetings with latency aged youth who are not old enough to engage in deep reflective discussion, they are not enough in themselves, and ways have to be found to deal with the conflict that is suitable for this age. This resonates with other findings (Rosen & Salomon, 2011). It could be that single-group meetings to work through impressions and difficulties with the "other" may be one solution. Inclusion of difficult subjects such as the political conflict in a mediated discussion may be another solution, and using the arts not just for mixing and positive experiences, but as a space to hold the conflict, may yet be another conclusion (Steele et al., 2002). We hope these findings will be of interest to group workers trying to lead multicultural or multi-ethnic conflict groups with latency children and for group workers working with diverse groups.

References

Bar-Tal, D. & Rosen, Y. (2009). Peace education in societies involved in intractable conflicts: Direct and indirect models. *Review of Educational Research, 79,* 557575

Ben Asher, S, Huss, E, Walden, Z., Sagi S, & Shahar, E. (2020). Perceived self-efficacy and hope of children in the Lesbos refugee school. *Journal of Refugee Studies, 3,* 30–45.

Ben-Ezer, G. (2002). The collective creative space as a tool with inter-cultural work: Group work with Ethiopian immigrants. In Kacen, L. & Lev-Wiesel R. *Group work in a multicultural society.* Tel Aviv: Cherikover Publications, 149–163. (Hebrew)

Benson, J. (1987). *Working More Creatively with Groups.* London: Tavistock Publications

Binder, J., Zagefka, H., Brown, R., Funke, F., Kessler, T., Mummendey, A., et al. (2009). Does contact reduce prejudice or does prejudice reduce contact? Longitudinal test of the contact hypothesis amongst majority and minority groups in three European countries. *Personality and Social Psychology Bulletin, 96,* 843–856.

Berger, R., Abu-Raiya, H., & Gelkopf, M. (2015). The art of living together: Reducing prejudicial attitudes through the Arab–Jewish class exchange program (CEP). *Journal of Educational Psychology, 107*(3), 678–688. http://dx.doi.org/10.1037/edu0000015

Biton, Y. & Salomon, G. (2006). Peace in the eyes of Israeli and Palestinian youths: Effects of collective narratives and peace education program. *Journal of Peace Research, 43,* 167–180. http://dx.doi.org/10.1177/0022343306061888

Brown, R. & Hewstone, M. (2005). An integrative theory of intergroup contact. *Advances in Experimental Social Psychology, 37*, 255–343.

Denzin, N. & Lincoln, Y. (2000). *Handbook of qualitative research.* California: Sage Publications.

Dewey, J. (1934). *Art as experience.* New York: Capricorn.

Erikson, E. H. (1982). *The life cycle completed.* New York & London: W. W. Norton.

Flum, H. (1994). *The Evolutive Style of Identity Formation.* Journal of Youth and Adolescence, *23*(4), 489–498.

Harel-Shalev, A. (2010). *The challenge of sustaining democracy in deeply divided societies: citizenship, rights, and ethnic conflicts in India and Israel.* Lanham, Maryland: Lexington Press.

Hickson, A. & Barker, C. (2002) *Creative Activities in Group work.* London: Routledge.

Huberman, M. & Miles, M. (2002). Reflections and advice. In. M. Huberman, & M. Miles, *The qualitative researcher's companion.* California: Sage Publications, 393–399.

Huss, E. 2012. *What we see and what we say: Using images in research, therapy, empowerment, and social change.* London: Routledge.

Huss, E., Kaufman, R., Avgar, A., & Shuker, E. (2016). Arts as a vehicle for community building and post-disaster development. *Disasters, 40*(2): 284–303.

Katz, Y. & Mayah, K. (1990). Reviewing dilemmas in facilitation of meeting groups between meeting groups of Arabs and Jews in Israel (Hebrew). *Megamot Lamed Gimel, 1*, 29–47.

Maoz, I. (2011). Contact in protracted asymmetrical conflict: Twenty years of planned encounters between Israeli Jews and Palestinians. *Journal of Peace Research, 48*(1), 115–152. http://dx.doi.org/10.1177/0022343310389506

Pettigrew, T.F. & Tropp, L.R. (2011). *When groups meet: The dynamics of intergroup contact.* Philadelphia, PA: Psychology Press.

Rosen, Y. & Salomon, G. (2011). Durability of peace education effects in the shadow of conflict. *Social Psychology of Education, 14*(1), 135–147. http://dx.doi.org/10.1007/s11218-010-9134-y

Steele, C. M., Spencer, S. J., & Aronson, J. (2002). Contending with group image: The psychology of stereotype and social identity threat. *Advances in Experimental Social Psychology, 34*, 379–440. http://dx.doi.org/10.1016/S0065-2601(02)80009-0

Steinberg, S. & Bar-On, D. (2002). An analysis of the group process in encounters between Jews and Palestinians using a typology for discourse classification. *International Journal of Intercultural Relations, 26*, 199–214.

Index

Note: Page locators in *italic* refer to figures.

www.ingramcontent.com/pod-product-compliance
Lightning Source LLC
Chambersburg PA
CBHW050438280326
41932CB00013BA/2162